AF292569

WHEN IN ROME

For Joel, for eternity

WHEN IN ROME

A NEW LOOK AT OLD GODS

LYNN HAMILTON

PEN & SWORD HISTORY

AN IMPRINT OF PEN & SWORD BOOKS LTD.
YORKSHIRE - PHILADELPHIA

First published in Great Britain in 2026 by
PEN AND SWORD HISTORY
An imprint of
Pen & Sword Books Ltd
Yorkshire – Philadelphia

ISBN 978 1 03613 607 9

A CIP catalogue record for this book is available from the British Library.

Typeset in Times New Roman 11.5/15 by
SJmagic DESIGN SERVICES, India.
Printed and bound in the UK by CPI Group (UK) Ltd.

The Publisher's authorised representative in the EU for product safety is
Authorised Rep Compliance Ltd., Ground Floor, 71 Lower Baggot Street,
Dublin D02 P593, Ireland.
www.arccompliance.com

For a complete list of Pen & Sword titles please contact
PEN & SWORD BOOKS LIMITED
George House, Units 12 & 13, Beevor Street, Off Pontefract Road,
Barnsley, South Yorkshire, S71 1HN, England
E-mail: enquiries@pen-and-sword.co.uk
Website: www.pen-and-sword.co.uk

or

PEN AND SWORD BOOKS
1950 Lawrence Rd, Havertown, PA 19083, USA
E-mail: uspen-and-sword@casematepublishers.com
Website: www.penandswordbooks.com

Contents

Author's Note

During the time your humble author should have been learning Latin, she was in love with teaching mythology to art students. So everything you read in this book is an interpretation of an English translation. And translations, themselves, become interpretations. While I have striven for accuracy, I have not tortured myself about the nuances of any particular Latin word.

Please also understand that this book is not comprehensive. It is, at best, an introduction to a subject that, in the past, people devoted whole scholastic lives to. I have clustered stories together around a character or an event, hoping to achieve a sense of continuity, with the Roman poet Ovid as my inspiration.

When determining whether an author is Greek or Roman, I simply used language. If they wrote in Latin, they were Roman. The Roman Empire was so extensive at one point, that this book features poets who were born in Africa and Spain. Some of the Latin-writing poets who acquired fame moved to Rome proper. Some did not. I have also quoted several English-language writers where their take on Roman myth was especially compelling.

This book may seem unfamiliar and wrong at times, because it cleaves to the Roman version in all things mythic. If you studied Homer's *Iliad* and *Odyssey* in college, this book may seem to contradict what you learned there. Homer's Odysseus is a Greek hero and a great humanitarian. But he is the enemy of the Trojans. Because the Romans identified with the Trojans, their Odysseus is a vicious criminal called Ulysses. He does not live happily ever after with Penelope. He is killed, and his son marries his father's former lover. Yes, Roman myth is often bleak.

Author's Note

Many scholars say that the Greek poets were the real, original thing. The Romans just copied them. And there is some truth to that. Around the time that BC gave way to AD, the Romans and their poets were busy 'syncretising' their religion.

That means they rewrote huge parts of the mythic stories that Rome absorbed from the Greeks, Etruscans, and north Africans, attempting to eliminate the internal contradictions and smooth out contradictory versions of the same sacred stories. Vase painters and sculptors contributed to this work. The aim was to have one consistent record of the stories that Rome used for self-identification. In the end, no such record exists, and readers must still navigate different versions.

The other point of view on Roman myth is that, in Roman poetry and fiction, the earlier Greek and Etruscan narratives found their finest and best expression. That is definitely the case with the sources I used for this book. Nothing is more beautiful than the poetry of Ovid and Virgil, and newer translations definitely hit the mark.

I feel the need to write a few words about the authors I discovered or rediscovered while writing this book.

Ovid

Ovid kept himself so hidden behind his words, we're lucky even to know that he had a daughter. He was a storyteller, perhaps THE storyteller. Maybe that's all we need to know, but it is so tempting to seek further information about the writers we admire.

One thing we know from Ovid's writings is that he wanted to backpedal on the human sacrifices. Time and again, in his *Metamorphoses*, a god spares a human's life at the last second or accepts an animal sacrifice in lieu of. According to his own *Fasti*, Ovid once spoke with the river god Tiber on the subject of human sacrifice versus using straw dummies of humans instead.

To prove that the gods did not require a live sacrifice, Ovid explained to Tiber that Hercules had swapped out straw effigies for sentient beings. And these non-sentient sacrifices were acceptable to the gods. Other devout observers followed Hercules' example.

(vii)

To settle the question of whether these fake sacrifices were acceptable to the gods, Tiber raised his waterlogged head, heavy with reeds, and addressed Ovid directly. Tiber explained that some of the Argonauts stayed behind on the hills descending to his river. One of them got homesick and asked that his dead, or nearly dead, body be thrown into the Tiber as a sacrifice and so that his body would roll back to his fatherland.

His descendant thought this expectation was unseemly and gave his ancestor a respectable burial in Ausonian soil, then threw a straw dummy into the river to represent his dead relative. The important part of this story is what happens next. Tiber lowers his head into an underwater cave, leaving the water undisturbed. *If* he had been dissatisfied with the straw man sacrifice, he would have at least rippled the water in disgust or sent up a tidal wave. By omission, the straw man is accepted as an honourable sacrifice, and no human sacrifices are required.[1]

It is clear to any careful reader, even in English translation, that Ovid wants to steer humanity toward rituals that can be performed without loss of human life or working animals. It is worth noting that the Judeo-Christian stories sometimes took a similar turn. In one scene from the Torah/Old Testament, God changes his mind about human sacrifice and stays Abraham's hand from killing his own son. Current scholarship says an earlier version of that story might have had Abraham going through with the murder. But the Holy Bible we use today pedals that violence way back and improves the Christian God's brand in the process.

Many Romans must have wished to scale back the sacrificial murders. In Ovid's fictional world, not by coincidence, the Roman gods are often placated with gifts of fruit, grain, and effigies. Ovid is careful to show that these farmed offerings are entirely acceptable to the gods on most occasions.

Ovid also ventured some cautious disapproval of the gods' behaviours – as he was writing about them. He notes that Neptune is cruel and profane when he rapes a young woman in a temple. He notes that Minerva punishes the innocent. He observes that Jupiter frequently lies to his wife.

This is where Ovid takes risks as a writer. He rewrites the gods as much as he can where the worship of them will endanger mere mortals.

And that is perhaps the reason that Ovid could not take risks anywhere else. Rewriting the gods, even a little, is dangerous in any religion. The texts of Christianity, for example, are carefully guarded with serious, damning curses for anyone who tries to add or subtract anything from the approved pages. The fatwah against Salman Rushdie is another example.

Modifying a god could even be construed as heresy. At the same time, it is always the poet's job to call out injustice. So we know little about Ovid personally, but we do know that he had some moral courage.

Was he an atheist? Julia Dyson Hejkuk writes that it is difficult to reconcile Ovid's wit, which frequently edges onto the limb of sarcasm, with any sincere belief in the divine. 'An unspoken syllogism runs as follows: Ovid is fun; religion is not fun; therefore, Ovid is not religious.'[2]

Readers do, generally, equate religious belief with sincerity in writing. But I have a different reason for believing Ovid was a non-believer – he had frequent divine revelations. According to his reports, especially in the more reverent *Fasti*, important gods visited him to clarify points of order. I'm trying to figure out how to say this politely: people who chat with one or more gods are often crackpots.

And yet no one in the universe seems more grounded than Ovid. You can't write like that without a clear head, unclouded by superstition. These god visitations point to atheism because only an atheist would invent a visit from the gods in order to make an important ethical point. And one wonders if that's what got him in trouble with authority.

At the age of 50, and after publishing his magnum opus, the *Metamorphoses*, he was banished from Rome and sent to rural Romania. There, he lived in a small settlement on the Black Sea, writing his last three long poems. He wrote cryptically about his banishment, saying that it was over a 'poem and a mistake'.

Scholars have long wondered what Ovid was punished for. Some speculate that the poet learned of Emperor Augustus' affair with his own daughter and didn't keep quiet enough about it. An inappropriate quip or lost poem on that subject would have been enough to incite an emperor's fury.

But, since we're speculating, what if he admitted to his religious scepticism? What if some witticism went just a little too far and betrayed the massive black hole where belief in the gods should be? I promise to write nothing further on this subject, dear reader, because it is the will of the universe that we shall never know what Ovid did to get himself exiled.

Ovid has a clever way of dealing with the various stories concerning gods, stories which sometimes clash or give alternate explanations for things. Instead of declaring one definitive version, he gives his readers options and asks them to decide for themselves. For example, the poet notes the existence of a small shrine to Minerva Capta and offers several different explanations for the link between the goddess and 'capital'. Is it because of her genius? Because she was born, fully-grown and armoured, from her father's 'caput', (i.e. head). Or is it because she endorses 'capital' punishment for stealing?[3] The poet never answers that question. He leaves it up to our imagination.

Leaving it up to the reader is a clever way to cover all the stories without seeming to introduce narrative incongruities. This technique again casts a doubt on Ovid's actual faith in the gods. If their attributes have several explanations, and there's no universal truth, how can we be sure any of the stories are real?

Virgil

Virgil's *Aeneid* is a book I have been reading for fifty years. Shadi Bartsch's translation was a revelation, and I felt that I was reading it for the first time. The main character's descent into the underworld is the most magical account of the supernatural.

Virgil was born near Pompeii, but he migrated to Rome to become a writer. While I'm on this subject, please know that modern scholars often use the 'Vergil' spelling, but I use 'Virgil' because it's how I was taught.

The classical hive mind thinks that Virgil definitely read Homer and was heavily influenced by the *Odyssey*. The Greeks had Homer and the *Odyssey* in which Odysseus travels all over the known world for twenty years. The Romans needed their own great traveller. In the *Aeneid*, the great ancestor of Roman emperors is tossed on the high seas for seven years.

Apuleius

Lucius Apuleius Madaurensis was also a revelation for me. His *Metamorphoses* or *the Golden Ass* is stunningly modern, all the more so for being unapologetically written in plain Latin prose. The characters read as if straight from the pages of any tabloid or perhaps a *Saturday Night Live* episode. Throughout this book, I have referred to his magnum opus as *The Golden Ass* to disambiguate it from Ovid's *Metamorphoses*.

Formerly despised as an African colonist, Apuleius is finally getting some of the recognition he deserves. His donkey has come to life and kicked the twenty-first century in its imagination. His new translator, Sarah Ruden, writes that his work is as entertaining as a 'groundhog in a frilly dress'.[4]

Apuleius was excluded from the canon of literary inquiry, at least in the 1980s, during what Joseph Farrell describes as the 'culture wars' of academia. The era of reading only dead white men is luckily over, Farrell writes. Well, maybe that's a very free paraphrase. What he writes, more precisely, is: 'there has . . . been a notable increase in the number of works that scholars study more or less for their own sake instead of for secondary purposes'.[5]

Seneca

Several plays by Lucius Annaeus Seneca, the Younger, were relevant to the story lines published herein. To read Seneca is to begin to understand stoicism. It's not just putting up with bad things. It's more a point of view that seeks true understanding and avoids assigning shame.

Seneca frequently puts his characters into opposition, each espousing a valid point of view. Rarely, if ever, does the poet declare one side the winner or on the 'right' side. This allows him to drill down into character motivations and reveal that there is no such thing as a classic villain.

Seneca was born and raised in southern Spain, near the town we have recently agreed to call Cordoba. He migrated to Rome to study rhetoric. Like Ovid, Seneca got himself into trouble with an emperor.

Claudius banished him to Corsica, but he was recalled to Rome to tutor a young Nero. He continued to advise Nero when the latter became emperor, and the first five years of Nero's reign were informed, at least in part, by Seneca's logic and clarity. But his influence waned.

We do not know if Seneca really participated in the assassination attempt on Nero; there may have been adequate reasons for wanting the end of that emperor. Nero was, by some accounts, a murderous tyrant who ended his second wife's pregnancy – and her life – by kicking her in the foetus. In any event, Seneca was found guilty and forced to commit suicide by drinking poison. He did so calmly, as befits a stoic.

Flacuus

No book on Roman myth would be complete without a dive into the *Argonautica* by Valerius Flacuus. It has been criticised as a clumsily written, incomplete saga of the golden fleece adventure. Despite that, it does gather up all the Argonauts, who steal the fleece with Medea's help and get away. It ends abruptly, but so does the *Aeneid*.

Flaccus' real achievement in the *Argonautica* is his portrayal of Medea's self-destructive obsession with Jason. Clearly still a teenager, she undergoes a transformation from self-possessed princess to crazy girlfriend in a matter of days. Raging adolescent emotions undo all her logic and composure.

Instead of attributing her change to teenage hormones, however, Flaccus shows us that it is the work of the gods. Every time Medea reasons her way out of her crush, Juno goes back to work on her, with the assistance of other goddesses. Flaccus didn't have the scientific studies to show how adolescent chemistry makes teens unstable, so he showed us how the gods destabilise their lives.

Hyginus

About the writer named Hyginus, scholars know very little. We may not even know his other names. He wrote a shortish encyclopaedia, called the *Fabulae*, that has no real literary ambitions. It is shamelessly prosaic, but extremely useful for filling in details missing from other sources. For the most part, the *Fabulae* is organised by people and events, but there are a few curveball entries.

Author's Note

The entry titled 'Exceptionally Handsome Men' seems oddly subjective, but it includes Tithonus, the mortal man so beautiful that Aurora, the goddess of the sunrise, fell in love with him. She asked the higher gods to make him immortal, and so they did. But Aurora failed to ask for eternal youth for Tithonus. In a few mortal years, he was no longer exceptionally handsome, but Aurora truly loved him, and she continued to rise from their shared bed, every day, to bring the dawn.

Other curiosities in the *Fabulae* are the list of Greek kings who participated in the Trojan War and how many ships each brought; the list of war heroes on each side and how many kills they had; and the list of 'Wives Who Killed Their Husbands'. Readers may or may not be surprised to learn that the list of 'Husbands Who Killed Their Wives' is only half as long.

All of the above sources deserve their own, separate study. I am only their humble curator.

Introduction

Belief in god(s) is a basic human need. But our religious needs today are not the same as in ancient Rome. Now, we have science. But what if we did not?

How would we explain the dying of the day, the dying of the year, the cycles of life and our planet? Since the time of ancient Rome, science has explained a great many things, such as the rotation of the sun and the aging process. But the Romans who built the first roads, aqueducts, baths, and security walls didn't have the comfort of an earth sciences textbook.

They needed the powerful beings of religious imagination to explain why the sky is red at dawn, why fermentation transforms grapes into an inebriant, why the world doesn't end when winter comes and the food sources die.

The story of Pluto and Proserpina explains why the world is warm one moment and freezing six months later. Pluto, god of the underworld, falls madly in love with Proserpina, daughter of the harvest goddess Ceres and kidnaps her. Ceres, whose good will powers agriculture, goes on a climate ravaging rampage, flooding and scorching the earth's food crops. In her grief, she brings humanity to the edge of starvation.

But the gods need humanity. Specifically, they need to be flattered and implored. That's how they were written. Eventually, deists would imagine a god that is indifferent to humans. But not the ancient Romans. Their gods were vain and petty, much more like tyrant kings and queens than supernatural beings.

They required temples and altars and sacrifices, huge investments of human time and energy. The smell of incense that accompanied prayer was exquisite to them. Prayers wafted upwards, towards their home in Olympos (frequently spelled 'Olympus') where they were pleased to be petitioned.

They mixed themselves up in human affairs with no worry about unintended consequences. With egos like that, the one thing the gods cannot collectively allow is the extinction of the human race. So Pluto brokers a deal with Ceres to share Proserpina. When she is with her mother, the world is spring and summer. When she is with Pluto, Ceres moderates her grief into a survivable winter.

Roman mythology is, first and foremost, a collection of stories like that one. The real-life ancient Romans understood the power of a unified belief system that relied on interesting narratives and crossed lines of race, language, and nation. Greek mythology was the most potent belief system in operation as Rome was rising. That meant that it behoved the Romans to absorb the Greek gods into the Roman pantheon rather than starting over with a new brand of religion or one that had only a regional following.

Rome fell, but its gods would remain in the fabric of our culture, popping up in every art form – paintings, sculptures, literature, even music – up to the present moment.

'If a face could launch a thousand ships, then where am I to go?' David Gates wrote in his iconic 1971 hit, 'If'. We listened to it on transistor radios and vinyl albums. Some of us had never heard a love song like that, one that vibrated with longing while making a classical allusion. The song laments the artist's limits, his inability to capture so big a love in art or in life.

Gates, a singer in the soft rock band, Bread, was writing about Helen, the Greek beauty that stole the heart of a visiting Trojan named Paris. When Paris spirited Helen onto his ship and sailed back to Troy, he started the Trojan War. It was epic.

Literally, it was the first epic, if you demand that your epics capture the spirit of an age, as they are meant to do. Gods, goddesses, battles, land monsters, sea monsters, narrow escapes, total destruction, and Deus ex machina happy endings for a few surviving warriors characterise the narrative of the Trojan war.

Greeks lay siege to Troy for ten long years, finally gaining entrance by way of the famous Trojan horse, then burning Troy to the ground.

Helen and her husband Menelaus survived the conflict and settled down happily, back in their home city-state of Sparta. With Paris dead on the field of war, Menelaus forgave Helen. After all, she could legitimately claim that 'Venus made me do it'.

Only later did the poets and painters wonder out loud about Helen. What kind of beauty could start a war of that magnitude? As the centuries galloped by, writers re-imagined Helen and Paris as a love story. That elusive longing for an emotional connection combined with lust and rebellion against convention captured the imaginations of both philosophers and readers. In Elizabethan England, playwright Christopher Marlowe described Helen of Sparta as 'the face that launched a thousand ships'.[1]

And that phrase stuck so hard that, around 400 years later, Bread casually threw the line in a song about a love that transcends time and the death of all the stars. Bread's 'If' struck such a nerve that musicians as dissimilar as Dolly Parton and Telly Savalas later covered it. If YouTube.com is any indication, people are still falling in love with 'If' and recording new versions.

That's why we need to remember the Roman myths. They are woven into the fabric of our culture, and almost no big picture is ever complete or perfectly understood without understanding them.

The Dei Consentes and Other Rock Stars

This is the place in any book on mythology where most mythologists will list the Dei Consentes with a tidy paragraph on each god's special powers. So I owe you an explanation as to why you will not see that list here. Not exactly.

The Dei Consentes are a rather arbitrary set of twelve powerful gods, six male, six female, that were related to Jupiter and Juno. The Roman poet and historian Livy introduced this concept of a twelve-god panel which is, in many ways, the model of a jury.

But that kind of list has limited uses for the reader who just wants to understand the basics of Roman myth. The Dei Consentes leave out some very powerful gods who were also related to Jupiter – Bacchus and Cupid, most notably. But the list does include deities that had little to do with what the Romans believed was their ancient history. Vesta, for instance, is consistently on the list. She is the goddess of the home and hearth, and she appears as rarely as she can in any action/adventure stories. Similarly, Vulcan, who is on the list of Dei Consentes, has almost no function in the war stories which are the backbone of Roman myth.

A list does not capture the way the Romans saw their gods. It captures the way we see those gods – as static icons in an alcove: curious, but almost entirely irrelevant to our daily lives. The modern western mind wants each god to have neatly defined characteristics, and to be doing a specific job.

But the Roman gods were not bureaucrats. They didn't have jobs or businesses. The concept of specialisation, so important to us, had no meaning to them. They were more like idle billionaires with a sociopathic edge. They were also an extended family who played by its own rules, and their dominant family trait was impulsivity.

Rome's ancient gods do not embody any set of ethics that most readers would affirm. They are more like the top TMZ celebrities: everything they do is interesting, but rarely are their actions kind or just. It can be truly shocking, especially to Christians who cleave to the New Testament and cross the street to avoid the old, to see powerful gods behave this way.

But as scholars have pointed out, the classical poets never equated the gods with morality, only with power. To put that another way, the ancients never asked the question 'What would Jupiter do?' because the answer would be 'Absolutely whatever felt good in the moment'.

Morality, for the ancients, was a moving target. Their gods were most certainly not role models. A code of relative ethics could only be deduced from a few human heroes who were elevated to the attention of these gods.

The poets, themselves, had the dubious honour of representing morality, whether they wanted the job or not. That's why Ovid was forever trying to steer the gods in the right direction, getting them to accept effigies instead of human sacrifices or, almost as bad, animals that humans needed for food.

All gods are the invention of humans, at least in your humble author's opinion. So, rather naturally, they mirror humanity. Often the Roman gods mirrored the worst humans: the angry, the violent, the sexual predators. Rarely did a god act alone. They ordered about the lesser gods – nereids, naiads, nymphs, satyrs – bribed their equals, and, when possible, tricked their betters. Lesser deities, like those that inhabited a single stream or forest, were more static and more inextricable from the resource they guarded.

But Jupiter, his siblings, and offspring were fully independent of any role they might happen to serve in the natural world. We think of them as having specific talents that they bestowed on humans, as they saw fit. But it would be more accurate to see them as rock stars with followers.

Let's say a young woman wanted to learn a stringed instrument. Apollo, god of the string section, would not descend and zap her with talent. No. She would pray to Apollo, she would make sacrifices, and, most importantly, she would practice. Then, if she was really lucky, Apollo might give her an opportunity to show how good she was.

Duality in Roman Myth

A simple portrait of the most powerful Olympian gods is best served by telling their stories. And the stories that cluster around the gods are often stories of duality. Historically, dualism has referred to the coexistence of spirit and body, but the Romans, especially Ovid, liked stories that featured co-stars doing related or opposite things. That's partly why there are so many twins in Roman myth: Castor and Pollux, Helen and Clytemnestra, Apollo and Diana, Romulus and Remus.

The two faced Janus is the most explicit example of this duality. Janus is a specifically Roman god, embodying duality all by himself with his two faces, facing in opposite directions, the original eyes in the back of a head. Janus is, officially, the god of beginnings and endings and transitions. For example, he watches the beginning of a conflict, then shows up at the end as well, to oversee the restoration of peace.

In the first book of the *Fasti*, Janus makes a personal appearance to Ovid in his home. The humble poet was hovering over his writing implements, wondering about the form and nature of Janus, when the room suddenly brightened and both Janus' faces were in Ovid's face.

The poet was terrified, he states, and his hair stood on end. But soon curiosity triumphed over fear as Janus answered the questions that were in Ovid's mind. Ovid pictures Janus with a skeleton key in one hand and a staff in the other. In this visitation, the god explains that he holds the key to everything in the heavens and on earth. Jupiter, the god of gods, passes through Janus' 'office' on his journey from heaven to earth and back again.

As an example of his power and duties, Janus notes that he is the one who ultimately confines war behind prison bars and beckons peace to leave her home and wander the highways of the world. Translators A. J. Boyle and R. D. Woodard bravely made a link between 'Janus' and 'janitor', indicating that Janus is a sort of all-purpose order maintainer. Janus also describes himself as a doorman and a quiet companion of the personified Hours, with whom he sits at heaven's entrance.

His role as gatekeeper of sorts explains why, though he is not an Olympian, Janus receives the first sacrifices of wine and incense. Janus, he self-reports, gives access to the other gods, and must therefore be propitiated. By his own admission, he is an old god, and his origin story goes back to the separation of the four elements. At the beginning of time, the elements of fire, water, earth, and air were commingled. Naturally, chaos reigned. Janus' shape as a god took form at the same time that the elements separated themselves out from the chaotic brew, and some semblance of the known universe took shape.

Among the things Janus is specifically responsible for is the start of every year. As many poets have done, Ovid pictures Janus as a vulnerable infant in the new year. It matters how this new year starts and how humans behave in January because that month sets the tone for the entire year. Boyle and Woodard use the word 'enervate'[2] to describe an undesirable state of lassitude that could overtake the world if the new year is not met with intellectual zeal. That's why Romans prosecute lawsuits on the first day of the year, Janus explains. At the start of the year, men must remember and state their worldly business in courts of law.

Another tradition that Janus oversees is the giving of new year gifts, especially gifts of dates, figs, honey, and straight up cash. Fruit and honey make the year glide sweetly forward, Janus notes, but then he lets rip a somewhat cynical note that cash is always sweeter than honey and that the race of men has become greedy and materialistic.

There's a longing for the past in Janus' meditations. He laments the new gods and their unseating of Saturn and the greed of new Rome. The ancient god complains that personified Justice no longer walks the earth because humans have driven her away.[3]

With only keys as his tools, Janus is not created for this new war-like humanity. Yet Janus presides over a doorway that leads to war. He does not start or encourage war, but he keeps this doorway open so that men can go to war, but also so they can return to peace. In peacetime, he locks the doors, so that peace will abide. Ovid works a quick compliment to Caesar here by having Janus say that the doors will remain locked for some time under the current Roman emperor.

PART I

THE ROYAL FAMILY

Chapter 1

Jupiter and Juno

Jupiter and Juno are perhaps the unhappiest married couple in all literary history. Jupiter is the 'king' of the gods, and all the most powerful deities in the pantheon are related to him one way or another. His sister, Juno, is his wife. She is, ever-so-ironically, also the goddess of marriage. Ironic, I say, because Jupiter is a player who takes a good deal of pride in his sexual liaisons both with other gods and humans.

Jupiter is linked to the sky, and he wields both thunder and lightning as weapons and distractions as needed. Whenever he wishes, he transforms himself into an eagle in order to survey the kingdom and spy on humanity.

Juno bore several powerful gods to her lawful husband, among them Vulcan, god of the forge and metal work. Apollo, Diana, and Mercury were born to Jupiter by other powerful goddesses. Venus was born from the sea, emerging fully adult, as pictured in the famous painting by Botticelli where she stands on a clamshell. She is technically the daughter of Saturn. She was conceived by the ocean when Jupiter cut off Saturn's testicles and threw them into the sea.

Much to Juno's dismay, Minerva was born to Jupiter parthenogenetically. She chiselled her way out of his skull, already an adult and dressed in defensive armour. Only in Ovid's poetry did Juno get even.[1]

In Ovid's world, Juno parthenogenetically conceived and gave birth to Mars, the most powerful war god. Other Roman writers thought Mars was the son of Jupiter and Juno. But the idea that Juno was one for one with Jupiter on parthenogenetic births is just too appealing to your humble author.

It might be difficult for a twenty-first-century reader to understand how anyone could worship a god like Jupiter and his relatives. We are used to our gods being violent warmongers, but not promiscuous. In the complex emotions that humans bring to religion, fear has always been an element. And the Romans managed to create fearsome gods that were arbitrary, egomaniacal, and greedy.

They were worshipped because they were feared, not because they were good role models. They were admired for the damage they could do. Laws were for humans and did not apply to gods.

Juno As Laughing Stock

The poets were careful not to mock Jupiter, no matter how much havoc he wreaked. His wife and sister Juno, however, did not enjoy that protection. She was unique in the pantheon as an easy target for poetic humour. She is forever trying to legislate something that can't be legislated: libido. She is the nagging sitcom wife of the pantheon.

Ovid would never dream of blaming Neptune for raping Medusa, nor Minerva for punishing Medusa unfairly. But, for some reason, the queen consort was ever a risible character. Perhaps the futility of her anger is what delights the Roman poets. Perhaps, women with cheating husbands are inherently comic, or perhaps it's how *often* Juno flies into a rage. The cycle of Jupiter's extracurricular affairs, followed by Juno's vengeance, and often the existence of a very inconvenient baby would be repeated many times with interesting variations.

Io was one of Jupiter's most famous extracurricular lovers. She was a nymph, the daughter of the powerful river god, Inachus. She was walking near that river when Jupiter saw her and praised her beauty loudly, telling her she should rest in the forest during the heat of the day. Io understood his intentions and she ran. Not to be defeated, Jupiter covered the earth in darkness to blind her, then raped her.

Juno noticed that day turned suddenly to night over Argos, and she knew something was afoot. 'Where was her husband?' Ovid writes.[2]

She descended to earth from Mount Olympos and reversed the day-to-night spell that Jupiter had cast. But her wily husband had anticipated her arrival and turned Io into a beautiful, white cow. Juno asked questions that Jupiter answered as cleverly as he could. This beautiful cow sprang from the earth, he claimed. Suspicious, Juno asked for the cow as a gift. Jupiter debated within himself whether he could afford to defy, not just his wife, but his sister, a near equal in power.

He gave the cow to Juno who put her under the supervision of Argus, a creature with a hundred eyes. He never closed all of them at once, so he was able to keep an around-the-clock vigil on Io. Argus grazed Io during the day, then crated her at night, putting her neck in a halter.

Whilst she was grazing, she happened upon Inachus, her father, and her sisters who did not recognise her, though they thought she was beautiful and allowed her to follow them. Finally, with a graceful hoof, she drew two letters of her name in the ground, and her father recognised her and wept. He had been searching for her.

But finding her transformed like this was worse than missing her, Inachus assured his daughter, and now he would prefer to die, though he was an immortal and the underworld was closed to him. Argus led Io away and positioned himself at the top of a slope where he could see everything with his wrap-around eyes.

The situation was intolerable, Jupiter felt. He needed someone to assassinate Argus, so he sent Mercury, who barely stopped to grab his pipe and don his flying sandals before obeying. Once in Argus' sphere, he played a tune on his pipe, and Argus invited the musician to his side.

Eventually, the messenger god lulled Argus to a full sleep, and all the eyes shut. Quickly, Mercury pulled out his rounded blade and killed Io's captor, hurling his body down a cliff. Predictably, Juno flew into a rage, and summoned a demon to drive Io crazy. In her madness, she ran to the Nile, fell to her knees on its bank, and begged the gods for mercy.

Jupiter took Juno into his arms and promised that the affair was over and that there would be no further consequences, perhaps meaning that there was no baby. Juno agreed to a detente, and Io was restored to her nymph form. She attained the status of goddess and had many worshippers. Few of Jupiter's lovers would fare so well.

Callisto, for instance, certainly did not seek out Jupiter's attention. She was a follower of the goddess Diana. As such, she had resolved never to take a lover, marry, or have children.

Virginity was a sacred state for Diana and her maidens. Like the other virgin huntresses, Callisto did not fuss with her clothes or hair, but carried a quiver and arrows as she hunted and played in the forest. She was napping in a spot of sun when Jupiter spotted her.

Cruelly, he disguised himself as Diana to get close to her. But when he gave her a non-platonic kiss, she tried to run. Rather heartbreakingly, Ovid suggests that, if Juno saw how hard Callisto fought against Jupiter, the queen might have been more merciful to his victim.

Callisto rejoined Diana's entourage where, formerly, she had been a favourite. But she declined to hunt side-by-side with Diana as she had in the past. Instead, she kept to the back of the followers, hoping to hide her sexual encounter.

Ovid imagined that there were a hundred ways to tell when a girl was no longer a virgin (something gynaecologists have absolutely confirmed you *cannot* do). But pregnancy, yes, that would give Callisto away when the girls gathered by a spring on a hot day.

By the time the other virgins had yanked her clothes off, it was obvious Callisto was having a baby. Diana banished her with no delay or sympathy, cutting the wound a little deeper by telling Callisto not to pollute the spring by touching it. Callisto named her baby boy Arcas, but Juno's anger with her was still fresh after the boy was born. She visited Callisto, calling her a whore and pulling her hair, then transformed the poor girl into a bear.

Years later, when Arcas was a teenager, he was hunting in the woods. He did not recognise his mother, but she recognised him, and she stared at him so meaningfully that he was terrorised and ran away. Nevertheless, it was only a matter of time before the boy would kill his own mother. Such a murder was a terrible offence against the gods, even when it was completely unwitting. So Jupiter turned both Callisto and her son into the constellations Ursa Major and Minor.

Jupiter's seduction of Europa is one of the most ancient of Roman myths, with a written record going back to the eighth century BC when she appears in the *Iliad* of Homer. She was a human princess of Tyre, the daughter of the Phoenician King Agenor. Jupiter had already spotted her and laid plans when he commissioned Mercury to drive Agenor's cattle down to the beach. Jupiter's plot would soon be manifest.

He knew that Europa liked to play on the beach with her friends. Once the cattle were there, he disguised himself as a beautiful white bull and mingled. He approached Europa in bull form, and she was surprised by his good looks and gentle manners.

She assembled a garland for his head, and he licked her hands in gratitude. Once she was no longer frightened of him, Jupiter pranced and frolicked with Europa like a dog with his owner. When she became brave enough to get on his back, he lost no time in swimming out to the middle of the ocean. Soon, he had landed on the shores of Crete, where he took a human form.

Europa gave her name to Europe because her brother, Cadmus, was sent to find a girl who was never to be found. Come back with her or don't come back, his father had said. Cadmus travelled everywhere looking for his sister. What he encountered, instead, was a dragon who killed all the men he was travelling with.

Cadmus killed the dragon, but in his loneliness, he became desperate and suicidal. He had been exiled from his family and homeland, now he was entirely alone. Minerva was his protector, so she instructed him to sow the dragon teeth in the ground like seeds. He did so, and a race of armed warriors sprang from the soil. They were so violent and aggressive that they fought each other to the death, and all of them but five were killed by the time they could achieve a truce. With these five men, Cadmus became the founder of Thebes, a city in south-central Greece.

The Backstory: Saturn and Ops

Jupiter and Juno didn't just wink into existence and start a race of gods. They have a solid backstory. Their parents were the titans, Saturn and Ops, creatures born out of chaos. In Roman myth, these titans ruled over a golden age in which the earth provided fruit and grain to humans who did not have to hunt or farm.

But Saturn, fearing that he would be overthrown by one of his descendants, proceeded to devour all his children. Ops, his wife, hid Jupiter the moment he was born and gave Saturn a rock to eat instead.

Saved by this deception, Jupiter grew up and, together with his siblings – Pluto, Neptune, Ceres, Juno, and Vesta – defeated their parents in battle and established themselves as the Olympians who ruled from Mount Olympos, a mountain so high that no mortal has ever ascended. The Olympians imprisoned many of the titans in an undisclosed location, often referred to as Tartarus, a section of the underworld.

Their imprisonment did not mean that mortals stopped celebrating them and even praying to them. Humans in real life celebrated the imprisoned Saturn during Saturnalia, an annual winter holiday for centuries before it gave way to Christmas.

The Working Titans

Not all the titans were imprisoned, however. The titan called Ocean continued to rule over the Atlantic, Arctic, and Pacific, roughly, and titan Hyperion continued to escort the sun across the sky. The titan Atlas was assigned to hold up the sky for eternity in some Roman sources. In others, he has the run of the Hesperides.

Prometheus, one of the titans, was permitted his freedom until he gave fire as a gift to struggling humanity. Then Jupiter punished him by chaining him to a cliff and having birds peck his liver. Janus, a late and specifically Roman god, was also a titan, the sibling of Saturn and Ops, and he worked directly with the new gods.

The titan, Latona, was also allowed her freedom. She was one of the younger titans, not born to Ops and Saturn. She was a beautiful goddess and, eventually, Jupiter noticed her. With Jupiter, she conceived twins, earning Juno's ire. These offspring would be the powerful gods, Apollo and Diana.

It is important to understand that the titans are always backstory. There was no time when the ancients worshipped the titans exclusively, and no texts that celebrate only the earlier generation of gods. The titanomachy, that ten-year war for dominance of earth, the underworld, and the heavens, was always part of the myth.

Humans never worshipped a free Saturn. Saturn was always in Tartarus, just as Elrond always fought against Sauron a thousand years ago, and just as Adam and Eve have always, already eaten that apple.

Chapter 2

Transformations

Who married Neptune? Some ancients say Tethys, the sea goddess. Others say Amphitrite, whose Roman equivalent was Salacia. Ovid solved this problem rather tidily by splitting the work of tending the salt water between two gods: the powerful and autonomous Neptune and 'Ocean', god of the 'encircling sea'.[1]

The encircling sea was the watery world outside the ancients' confined realm of Greece, Rome, the middle east, Turkey, and north Africa. Today we would call the encircling sea 'the Atlantic, Pacific, Russia, China, Australia, the north and south poles, and North and South America'. Or maybe just 'the rest of the world'. The ancient world of the poets was a small fraction of what we actually have.

The existence of the titan Ocean, who was married to Tethys, freed Neptune up to marry Amphitrite. It also freed him to be a much more fully-fledged character, with the complex needs of a human and the absolute power of nature. Ovid's Neptune is as capricious as Jupiter. Like Jupiter, he acts on grudges, largely unguided by morality or empathy. The sea is his plaything. If he dislikes the captain of a ship, he kicks up a storm. But only he is allowed to act out in that way. If the sea is riled without his permission, he calms it. Like his brother, he pursues minor goddesses and mortal women ruthlessly for sex.

Early in the history of gods and humans Jupiter and Neptune were angry with the way civilisation was going. Humans were corrupt and insufficiently respectful of the gods. Jupiter wanted to set fire to the entire earth, but in conferring with the other gods, he decided it was safer to flood the earth than to set it aflame.

So he released the rains of heaven on the earth. Neptune, god of the water, joined him and let the river banks and seas overflow, adding catastrophe to disaster. In this action, Jupiter and Neptune mirror the anger of the Old Testament god who arrived at the same manner of punishing depravity. Most of humanity perished, of course, their only recourse to climb higher. Sea creatures swam where formerly there had been human habitats:

> The woods are invaded by dolphins,
>
> blundering into the branches and bumping the trunks till they shake them.
>
> Wolves are swimming among the sheep.[2]

When Jupiter looked down and saw earth submerged in water, with most of humanity drowned, he relented and stopped the storm. Neptune called on his son, Triton, to calm the seas. Triton was a merman – his upper half man, his lower half fish – who played a magic trumpet or bugle. With his instrument, he played a song, heard around the world, that told the waters to withdraw. The streams returned to within their banks and other waterways followed suit. Deucalion and Pyrrha, two virtuous, humble humans, were left to repopulate the earth.

After the Flood

Another story surrounding Neptune has him hiking with Jupiter and Mercury. They were spotted by a very poor farmer. This man, Hyrieus, offered the gods his hospitality, thinking they were mortal travellers. They accepted only upon repetition of the invitation.

The farmer served wine to Neptune, who told their host to serve Jupiter next. Upon hearing the name of the father god, the farmer started shaking with panic. He was all in, though. He had exactly one farm animal, an old ox that ploughed his small plot. This animal Hyrieus killed and roasted as an entree for his godly visitors. He also broke out the good wine that he had been saving since he was a child and served it.

This story illustrates how much of religious belief is about fear. Without an ox, the old man would effectively have grown his last crop.

He was, literally, facing starvation to honour these powerful beings that he had mistaken for ordinary, weary travellers.

Luckily, the gods received Hyrieus' little all with gratitude. 'Ask for what you want', Jupiter told him. The farmer should have asked for a lifetime supply of corn and grapes. Instead, he wished for a son, and the gods provided him, once again, with a child not born of woman. Ovid is embarrassed about the details of Orion's origins, but he implies that Hyrieus ejaculated into the ground. The gods blanketed the wet spot with soil, then ten months later, a boy was born. His name was Urion, which was changed to Orion.

The goddess Delia made Orion her companion and guardian, but Orion angered the gods by bragging about his own strength. There was no monster alive that he could not defeat, he claimed. Such bravado rarely goes unpunished in Ovid's universe. The gods sent a scorpion, which went after Delia herself. Orion blocked the scorpion's sting and was rewarded by turning into a star.

Winter to Spring

The gifts of Ceres are there for all to see: crops, harvests, a full table groaning with the weight of food. Early humans had nothing to eat but raw vegetables, mostly grass, then they discovered acorns, and that improved their diet substantially.

But Ceres, goddess of agriculture, was generous. She introduced humans to farming, showing them how to grow food intentionally and yoke the steer to a plough. Eventually, humans used copper and iron in forging their farming implements.

On a regular day, Ceres travelled to Henna to attend a feast. She was accompanied by her daughter, Proserpina, and several other girls who enjoyed running across Henna's fertile meadows. Proserpina found a waterfall and a meadow of colourful flowers which she commanded her entourage to gather.

In her zeal to gather a really amazing bouquet, Proserpina wandered a short distance from her friends. Pluto, god of the underworld, saw the young goddess, reined up his horses and ascended to the earth's surface just long enough to grab her and drag her down to his kingdom which poets variously call 'hell' and 'Hades' and 'the underworld'. It is the world that people enter when they die.

The kidnapping of Proserpina turned into a wedding, making the bride the queen of the underworld. By the time Ceres learned what happened, Proserpina was linked to Pluto in a marriage that had all the earmarks of a noble coupling. This would become a diplomatic problem.

Ceres ransacked the known world – Europe, Asia, and Africa – searching for her lost daughter. In her hands, she carried two pine trees, lit with flames, as her torches. The world turned dark; it was everlasting night for humans while Ceres mourned the loss of her child. The crops failed, humans starved. When she came to the sea, she hitched snakes to her chariot and continued searching. In time, she rested on a rock in Greece, and mourned for several days straight.

Here, she was found by a farmer named Celeus and his small daughter. As poor as those two mortals were, they had each other, and Ceres told Celeus that he was luckier than she. Celeus and his daughter were kind hearted, and they joined Ceres in weeping over the loss of Proserpina. Ceres accepted Celeus' kind offer of hospitality at his tiny hovel.

There, she met Metanira, Celeus' wife, and their baby son who was dying. Ceres saved the boy by placing her mouth on his. The family rejoiced and set out a modest feast of apples, honey, and cottage cheese. Ceres was not quite done blessing this family, but things fell apart when she tried to give the formerly sick boy, Triptolemus, immortality by burying him in the live embers of the fire. His mother woke and grabbed him from the fire instinctively.

Offended, Ceres flew off, noting that the child would remain mortal, but she held no further malice. It was the sun god who finally told Ceres, bluntly, that her daughter was now the bride of Pluto and Queen of the Underworld. 'Ask Jupiter', he said.

So Ceres confronted Jupiter, demanding satisfaction, and reminding Jupiter that Proserpina was his daughter. Jupiter had to point out that Pluto wasn't the worst son-in-law she could have; he was nearly equal in status to Jupiter and Neptune. The three gods were brothers and Ceres was their sister.

Proserpina had now married a man who was her uncle on both her mother's and father's side. But neither Jove nor Ceres was much worried about the incest, which would be a good enough reason to cancel the marriage today. Instead, whether Proserpina was a true citizen of hell was determined by whether she had eaten anything in that country from which no mortal returns. Alas, an investigation concluded that she had eaten three pomegranate seeds. Those seeds anchored her to the underworld.

Ceres prepared to immigrate to the underworld herself. But that would have left the world in darkness and famine! So Jupiter did what he does best, and performed a little ex machina. Rules there may have been about who belongs in heaven, who in hell. But Jupiter declared that Proserpina would spend half her time with her mother, during which humans grow and gather their crops, and half her time in the underworld with her husband.

Few, if any, stories, tell us how Proserpina felt about this treaty. But, upon her first return to Ceres' world, the human realm was blessed with bumper crops of corn and grapes. The barns could barely contain so much bounty.[3]

Grapes Into Wine

Bacchus is a puzzling and inconsistent creature. His story begins when Jupiter spies the beautiful Semele, a human princess, the daughter of the great Cadmus. Jupiter always disguised himself to make love to mortal women; this time, he took the form of a mortal man, not so different from the other mortal men Semele had seen. Soon she became pregnant with Bacchus, who would become the god of wine, frenzy, madness, and inspiration.

Ovid wastes few words on the affair and, instead, focuses on Juno's furtive anger. First she convinced herself that there was no point confronting Jupiter. To be fair, it had done no good in the past. And there had been many affairs already in their long marriage.

The reader can see her self-esteem crumbling as her monologue wears on: 'If I am to merit/the title of mighty Juno; if I may properly wield/my jewelled sceptre as Queen of the Gods; if I am Jupiter's sister and consort – at least his sister!'[4] The only correct course of action was to take her anger out on the girl, Juno reasoned.

As any woman knows who has been publicly betrayed in her marriage, the disrespect is the worst of it. But there was no way to cure the underlying problem. Jupiter could and would make mortal babies with precisely as many beautiful girls as he cared to.

So Juno disguised herself as an old woman who looked like Semele's childhood nanny. In this guise, she insinuated herself into Semele's presence. Semele, an open-natured girl, quickly took Juno into her confidence.

The goddess convinced Semele that Jupiter didn't really love her as much as she – Semele – thought. Semele should ask Jupiter to make love to her in his true form, the form he takes when he beds his wife, Juno advised from within her deep cover. After all, many ordinary men have tricked women into unwed sex by claiming they were gods, Juno insinuated.

The next time Jupiter visited her, Semele first asked him for a favour. Reckless, not knowing what she would ask for but confident it was something easy for him, he swore by the River Styx to grant her any wish. Such an oath is binding, even on the high god of Olympos.

When Semele asked him to reveal his divine form, he sighed, knowing that such a request would kill her. He ascended to heaven, gathering dark clouds and rain around him to buffer his radiance. He left his lightning bolt on a shelf. He descended to earth again, hoping that the clouds in which he swathed himself would shield his lover, but knowing they would not.

Finally, he revealed himself to Semele, and she burst into flames. Mortals are not meant to look on the gods in their raw form. Jupiter could not save her, but he snatched her baby boy out of Semele's womb and stitched the foetus up in his own thigh, where the baby gestated to full term. The infant Bacchus was born directly from Jupiter, who gave him to Semele's sister, Ino, to raise. Soon Ino would hide him with the nymphs to be raised to adulthood.[5] Bacchus wears a crown of leaves, not because they are grape vines, but because, when he was very small, one of his guardians put him in a basket covered with ivy to hide him from a vengeful Juno.

Somehow, March 17, which is known in the western world as Saint Patrick's Day, used to be the official day to celebrate Bacchus in ancient

Rome. In honour of Bacchus, boys would receive an adult toga, the 'toga of liberty',[6] perhaps because Bacchus often looks like a boy on the verge of adolescence.

While officially the god of wine, inspiration, and madness, Bacchus has moments of acting like a responsible adult, as when he rescues and marries Andromeda, then bestows immortality on her. At other points, Bacchus is a carefree bachelor roaming the countryside in the company of satyrs and their ancient father, called only 'the old man' in A. J. Boyle's translation of the *Fasti*, but often identified as Silenus, the biological ancestor of the satyrs.

Silenus was both godfather to the satyrs and god of drunks. Yes, I hear you saying, 'but the Romans already had a drunk god in Bacchus'. What can I tell you, dear reader? The Canadian Inuits have around twenty-four words for snow. The ancients had multiple gods for various stages of inebriation. We diversify where we have a particular expertise.

Silenus became prophetic when drunk, and he was always drunk, to the point where he needed a donkey or a number of volunteer satyrs to keep him upright. Bacchus' travels with Silenus were always accompanied by the music of hand cymbals, played by the satyrs.

Satyrs were under the nominal protection of Bacchus, whom they followed around like groupies. There really is no delicate way to put this, so I'm just going to use the language of therapy here: Satyrs were sex addicts and alcoholics. If you were a painter in the Middle Ages who wanted to get an R-rating for your painting, you would throw in an erect satyr, looking lecherously at a circle of half-clad maidens.

The satyrs were unreliable, if not fickle, by nature. It is always a mistake to ask them for help. The ancients portrayed these playboys as mostly human with horse-like facial features. Only in later centuries did they show up with goat legs.

In addition to being every discount hotel's worst nightmare, Bacchus is also a farmer, of sorts. He is certainly the god that ancient grape growers would pray to. He also introduced honey to the larger world by trapping a hive of bees in a tree.

It is worth noting that honey is the chief ingredient in mead, a refreshing alcoholic beverage that the ancient world often relied on for its buzz. Silenus once attempted to keep the location of a honeycomb a secret, but honey and mead are to be shared. So Silenus got badly stung by bees and then kicked by a donkey.[7]

Virgil's *Georgics*, a book on the gods and farming, praises Bacchus and wine making. Raptures to the wine of the gods alternate with good practical advice to growers, that can be roughly translated, 'Orchardmen! Learn the science of growing a specific species of fruit! Plant intensively! Cultivate! Tame wild plants!'[8]

Mercury and Minerva

Mercury has been dubbed the 'messenger god', which is very deceptive. Mercury is not a simple courier; he is more high-end butler to Jupiter. Jupiter has flight and even a limited form of ubiquitousness in his repertoire of powers. But, unlike the omnipresent 'one true god', the Olympians were unable to be everywhere, all the time. Also, unlike the god of the monotheists, they were not necessarily able to do two or three things at the same time.

Jupiter often delegated when there were multiple elements to one of his schemes. So Mercury helped Jupiter, especially with Jupiter's affairs. In many ways, Mercury is like an assistant dean of the gods to Jupiter's deanship. A student of Roman myth might be tempted to say, 'Like father, like son'. Like Jupiter, Mercury is a merciless sexual predator, liar, and trickster. Worshipping Mercury was risky. He might reward cunning behaviour, or he might not.

A story that illustrates Mercury's character is that of Battus. Battus was an old horse herder who observed Mercury stealing and sequestering some of Apollo's cattle. Mercury bribed the old man to pretend he had not seen the theft. In return for Battus' discretion, the god gave him one fine steer. Most importantly, Battus was not to say where the stolen cattle were. Battus assured the god of his compliance, pointing to a rock and declaring that the rock would talk before he would.

Then, as a test of character or perhaps just because he was bored, Mercury withdrew, disguised himself and rounded on Battus, asking where the stolen cattle were and offering another bribe. Battus was quick to point in the direction of the herd, and Mercury revealed himself, taunting Battus. He had betrayed Mercury to Mercury, the god said, laughing. Then he turned Battus into a stone, similar to the stone he had sworn by.[9]

Mercury never married, though there was certainly a precedent for powerful gods to have wives. Jupiter, Neptune, and Pluto were husbands. Even Bacchus and Cupid had wives. Like Jupiter, Mercury had his share of affairs, and he took women by force on more than one occasion.

In Prague's famous castle hangs a fresco of Mercury and Minerva from the sixteenth century. It was painted by Bartolomeus Spranger, and it portrays the two gods against a blue backdrop that evokes the heavens. The painting is useful to students of Roman mythology because it captures many of the symbols that both poets and artists used to identify the ancient deities. Minerva has her helmet, shield, and owl. Mercury has his caduceus – a sort of sceptre, as well as wings on his sandals and helmet.

Offhand, it's hard to think of any two popular Roman gods who have less in common, but the odd artist liked to pair them up, perhaps for the very reason that they were so unalike. Minerva, especially in her later incarnations, is the goddess of wisdom, study, virtue, and self-discipline. Mercury is morally VERY sketchy, impetuous and a prankster who enjoys a good laugh at others' expense.

Minerva's character is best revealed in her relationship to Ulysses, especially in his return to Ithaca after the Trojan War. So this chapter will not attempt a full character analysis. Minerva's overall seriousness, in stark contrast to Mercury's whimsy, was her prevailing condition. That seriousness probably explains why she was the patron god of Athens, the ancient world's beating heart of art, science, and imagination. That does not mean that she could not be cruel. She was extremely inhumane on more than one occasion.

The Minerva that humans celebrate today – she of the toga and owl – has come to represent wisdom and civilised conduct. That's why J. K. Rowling named a pivotal character in the Hogwarts world after this goddess. She was not always thus; the ancients revered a Minerva that was frequently impulsive and lacking in a sense of proportion.

But Alfred Tennyson and his poet peers of the nineteenth century rewrote Minerva as the embodiment of logic and self-discipline. In one of his narrative poems, the goddess defines her sphere in these words:

Self-reverence, self-knowledge, self-control,
These three alone lead life to sovereign power…
And because right is right, to follow right
Were wisdom in the scorn of consequence.

Minerva goes on to note that she doesn't believe in bribing her followers, but:

. . . my vigor, wedded to thy blood,
shall strike within thy pulses like a God's,
To push thee forward thro' a life of shocks,
Dangers, and deeds, until endurance grow
Sinew'd with action . . .[10]

Mercury and Minerva are thrown together in the story of Herse, a beautiful priestess of Minerva herself. She lived in a three-room apartment with her sisters, Aglauros and Pandroso. The three of them were in charge of protecting a box for Minerva. They were to keep the box safe, the goddess had explained, but they were not to look inside it. Was Minerva actually embarrassed about what the box contained? She should not have been, but there's a good chance she was.

Minerva had recently had occasion to visit her brother Vulcan in his dark underground smithy. Hard to say what he was thinking, but Vulcan was suddenly possessed of an uncontrolled lust for Minerva. She fled his embrace, but he shot off some semen that landed on her thigh.

She shook it off with revulsion, but the semen then inseminated the soil which conceived a boy. With the prescience of gods, Minerva knew this boy would one day be king of Athens. So she saved Neptune's son, and put him in a box to keep him safe. She placed her priestesses in charge of it with the orders that they should never, ever open the box. At some point, Aglauros had violated Minerva's order and peeked inside.

Shortly thereafter, Mercury spotted Herse, Aglauros' beautiful sister and fellow priestess. He took a moment to straighten his robe and smooth his hair before approaching the sisters in a straightforward manner. He entered their home and introduced himself to Aglauros. To her, he announced his intention of making love to Herse.

To understand what happened next, we must understand that a visit from a god was a tremendous honour, the greatest a human could expect, even when the god's intent was to prey on a young woman. And Mercury hadn't disguised himself too thoroughly; he looked like the god he was.

Aglauros' behaviour was, therefore, outrageous. She demanded a huge tribute of gold before she would give Mercury access to her sister and kicked him out of the house until he could produce it. It was quite a bit like asking Brad Pitt to pick up the cheque when he joins you for dinner.

Minerva, who had been watching this exchange, huffed in fury. She knew that Aglauros had profaned her duties by spying Vulcan's baby. And now she would have a famous sister! And Mercury would be indebted to her! And she would be rich with all that gold!

To today's savvy reader, it sure sounds like Minerva herself was stricken with jealousy. But Ovid, who liked to scoot right along the edge of blasphemy, doesn't say so. Instead, he has Minerva descending into a cold, dank valley that never feels the warmth of the sun.

There she found the goddess Envy, a withered pale creature, grotesquely skinny, with decaying and discolouring teeth and poor eyesight. Her nipples were green and her mouth drooled poison. Only the sight of pain could make her smile. Her unending resentment made her an insomniac. Envy was literally gnawing away at her from within.

Minerva found this creature feasting on snakes; it was the way she renewed her supply of venom. Envy, Ovid notes, is a self-inflicted torture. Of course she noticed how healthy and attractive Minerva looked. Her armour would have gleamed had there been any light in Envy's sunless existence.

Minerva stated her business without delay. Aglauros must be poisoned. Then the goddess of defensive arts and wisdom launched herself back up to heaven, tapping her spear tip on the chamber floor for emphasis.

Envy arose from her private hellscape and approached Athens, poisoning whole cities with her toxic breath as she travelled. Grass withered at her feet and she maliciously destroyed tree tops. She took a moment to look on Athens and almost wept. It was, at that moment in time, a haven for talent, wealth, and peace. There was nothing to delight her in the sight of it.

She found Aglauros asleep and reached a rusty hand toward the girl's heart. Envy stuffed that heart with brambles. That popular tattoo, of a heart wrapped in barbed wire, comes to mind. Envy's poison breath seeped into Aglauros' lungs and bloodstream.

The toxic goddess also put images in her victim's head: here was a picture of the handsome Mercury; here was a picture of Herse as a happy bride – even though Mercury had said nothing of marriage. Her resentment was like an invisible, smouldering fire. Soon, Aglauros was so crazy that she lost her sense of basic self-preservation. She squatted in front of Herse's door, blocking Mercury's way.

Mercury, up to this point, had been surprisingly good natured. But you do not come between an ancient Roman god and what he wants. To be fair, he did try to charm Aglauros out of the way first.

'I won't budge from here until you pack up and go away', was approximately what she said in reply.

In his own way, Mercury granted this wish. He touched his wand to Herse's door which swung open fast. Aglauros tried to rise, but the blood in her veins went white as, on the outside, she turned to black stone.[10]

Apollo and Diana

Apollo and Diana are twins and the outcome of Jupiter's affair with Latona, a beautiful titan from a recent generation of the old gods. Latona was not a part of the ten-year-war between the old gods and new. Her affair with Jupiter was typical of his dalliances. He saw her on the sly, making Juno furious.

When it came time for Latona to deliver her babies, Juno pursued the poor titan everywhere, never letting her settle, ensuring that everyone turned her away. In her desperation, Latona found the island of Delos, which was attached neither to the mainland nor to the seas. There, she gave birth to Apollo and Diana who share a love of hunting, especially archery.

Diana's field of play is the forests where she frolics, hunts, and swims with a band of her fellow virgins. One story, beloved of artists and sculptors, further underlines how protective Diana was of her own privacy and that of her tribe.

There was a pine and cypress forest sacred to Diana. In this forest were a cave and grotto in which she liked to bathe with her followers. One day, she and a small group of maidens were naked and bathing when Actaeon, grandson of Cadmus, happened upon them. He had been hunting when he stumbled into this magical grove, and he wandered therein, distracted.

When the young women saw him, they screamed, their voices echoing through the wood. They circled Diana to hide her, but she was taller than all the rest, so her naked neck and shoulders were visible. Ovid's Diana would have liked to shoot him herself, but she was bathing, with no bow or arrows to hand. So, instead, she threw water in Actaeon's face and uttered a curse: 'Now you may tell the story of seeing Diana naked – if storytelling is in your power'.[11]

It is not clear whether it was her words or the water cast in his face that transformed Actaeon. He sprouted antlers first, then his hands turned into hooves, his arms into forelegs, his ears lengthened and pointed. Suddenly, he was covered, not in smooth skin, but a deer's fur. He had been transformed into a stag.

But Diana's final blow was to give him the stag's fear and panic. As soon as his metamorphosis was complete, he bolted, galloping through the woods. He did not realise he was a deer, so his sudden speed surprised him. He still had all the consciousness of a human. He came to a pool of water and saw himself.

Then he knew, and tears coursed down his rough coat. He attempted a cry to heaven, but all that came from the stag's mouth was a howl. He stood there, ashamed, debating whether he could go home, when his own hunting dogs got a whiff of him. Dogs with names that Raeburn translates as 'Hurricane', 'Tracker', 'Ravenous', and 'Fawnkiller' did not recognise their owner.

The dogs chased Actaeon over hill and dale until three canines took a short cut over a ridge and brought him down. The others caught up and tore him apart. Actaeon's friends, who had been hunting with him, saw the savagery and cheered the dogs on. There was some debate amongst the gods about whether Diana might have gone too far, but Juno was secretly pleased because she hated the house of Cadmus. She was still bitter over her husband's seduction of Europa, Cadmus' sister.[12]

Like his twin, Apollo is talented with bow and arrows. He is also a patron of the arts, especially music, poetry, and dance. He is god of whatever medicine the ancients had at their disposal. As the god most closely associated with prophecy, he established the oracle at Delphi where a human priest or priestess exists to tell the future to petitioners. He is also the god of light.

Ovid tells the story of Apollo's pipe playing competition with Pan. It's a story that illustrates the overlapping nature of the gods' spheres. Pan was an important god, though not as powerful as the Olympians, and he is often pictured by artists with the furry legs of goats and playing on pan flutes, which are actually named after him.

Pan is roughly the god of rural joys; he presides over meadows, woods, and glens. Though he is not as crudely portrayed as Priapus, he is interested in sex and often hears prayers for conception. He keeps company with nymphs.

On one occasion, Pan got to bragging to some nymphs about how well he played his pipes. Then he went a step further and challenged Apollo to a competition. Apollo accepted the challenge, and the musicians agreed that Tmolus, a mountain god, would judge the contest.

Pan went first and he produced a sound that Raeburn translates as 'barbarous'. Apollo went next. The lyre was his instrument, and it was inlaid with ivory and gems. When he had played his tune, Tmolus declared him the winner, as did everyone else who had been listening, except for Midas who happened to be eavesdropping. He preferred the rough sound of the pipes. For his minority opinion, Apollo turned Midas' ears into those of a donkey.[13]

On another occasion and fresh from killing a serpent that had been ravaging the countryside, Apollo ran afoul of Cupid, Venus' son by Mars. Ovid's Cupid remained a child, so when Apollo saw his bow and arrows, he mocked him for playing with adult weapons.

And he didn't stop there. He praised his own accomplishments in archery, citing the monster he had just killed. Cupid had no business with weapons that Apollo had made great, was the gist of this banter.

Cupid did not take these jibes in the spirit of jest. He loaded two arrows, one tipped with gold and one tipped with lead. The gold arrow would inspire an uncontrollable lust and the lead arrow would make the thought of sex revolting.

He shot Apollo with the gold arrow and he developed a raging passion for Daphne, the daughter of a river god, Peleus. Cupid then shot Daphne with the lead-tipped arrow. Daphne, an informal follower of Diana, had already turned down many suitors. She liked to dress casually, put her hair up, and run through the forests.

This was mildly disappointing to her father who would have liked grandchildren. But one day, Daphne told her father that she preferred the life of a virgin, and she invoked the example of Diana whose father, Jupiter, allowed her to live unmarried. Peneus granted her wish to remain single.

Ovid compares Apollo's state of mind to a burning hedgerow that was set on fire by a careless worker's torch. The poet notes that Apollo is the god of prophecy and should have been able to see where this destructive passion would lead. But even that gift could not save him. Cupid's infection gave no quarter and could not be reasoned with.

When she saw Apollo pursuing her, Daphne ran. Apollo called out to her that he was not the enemy, but the great god Apollo. He recited his resume as he chased her. He brought music! Poetry! Archery! Healing! Herbalism! Then, parenthetically, he noted that no herbs could save him now.

He asked her to slow down; he was afraid she would hurt herself and scratch those beautiful arms and legs. She did not slow down. She ran faster, but she was running from a god. Soon his breath ruffled the hairs on the back of her neck.

Through a break in the trees, she saw her father's river, and she prayed to him to transform her. In an instant, she had grown bark across her chest, her arms became branches, her feet became roots, and her hair became the leaves in a tree canopy. Daphne was now a laurel, and Apollo was thwarted.

He hugged and kissed the tree in sorrow. Cupid had shot his arrow into a young god's virgin heart. Daphne was his first love, so he wound the leaves of her into a wreath for his head, and he wore that wreath forever. Laurel leaves, to this day, symbolise achievement and leadership in the Apollonian tradition.[14]

The Fates

Jupiter is god, or so it might seem, but there were women he quietly obeyed. The three women behind the gods were called Parcae. Together they represented inexorable fate.

Where they lived is a mystery. They were not on Olympos with the Dei Consentes. Some writers thought they occupied a corner of the underworld. They were pictured most often in a small cluster, spinning. The threads they handled represented individual human lives. When a thread was cut, that individual's life ended, and there was no retracting it. To that extent, even Jupiter's power was constrained by these females.

The poets wrote very little about the Parcae. Though they were immortal, their stories hold little interest. They are forces of the universe, immoveable, but with little personality. They do not engage the world on any level. They have no direct contact with humans or even with the other gods.

Even those heroes who visit the underworld never see them. For all their power, they live much like books on a shelf or rocks on a beach. We don't know what they think about when they are not working – if, in fact, they think at all. They manage mortal lives, but they seem to have no agency over their own destinies.

When it comes to death, however, they are absolute. When they cut the thread of Sarpedon's life on the Trojan battlefield, even Jupiter could do nothing to stop it. And Sarpedon was Jupiter's beloved son.

Chapter 3

The Lovers

The mild eroticisation of the gods might be one of the things that distinguishes Roman myth from Greek and makes Ovid more fun to read than Homer. Ovid wrote a scene in which Jupiter asked Juno: Who enjoys sex more? Men or women? Jupiter theorised that it was women, but Juno disagreed.

So they consulted Tiresias because he had experienced life as both a man and a woman. He had been walking in the woods when he saw two snakes mating. For no disclosed reason, he struck them with his staff, but did not kill them. Suddenly, he was transformed into a woman.

He remained in the shape of a woman for seven years, then saw the same snakes having sex and struck them again. The magic worked; he was a man again. Tiresias settled the dispute in Jupiter's favour. Yes, women actually enjoy the act more, he affirmed.

One hopes he was prepared for Juno's wrath. She struck him with blindness, a curse that Jupiter could not undo because of strict laws that say a god cannot undo the work of another god. To counteract Juno's vicious anger, the best Jupiter could ever do was award a compensatory gift. To Tiresias, then, he gave the gift of seeing the future. He became a powerful prophet, known for telling Ulysses how to survive the journey home to Ithaca.

Mars and Venus

Botticelli's *Venus and Mars* is one of the most beautiful paintings in the world. It shows the two gods in private repose: he sleeping, she resting. They are reclining in a bower, the kind of place that lovers repair to when they wish to have illicit sex. In the background are childlike creatures with small horns and the legs of animals, possibly fauns. They are playing with Mars' weapons, confident that he won't wake, or that they won't be punished if he does.

Botticelli painted *Venus and Mars* during his mythic period, a time that is frequently recognised for his best work, art curator Caroline Campbell explains, in a lecture on the painting. It is part of a series that includes *The Birth of Venus* and *Spring*. In *Venus and Mars*, Mars is definitely sleeping the sleep of the man who came straight home after a battle and made love to Venus.

'You can tell that he's snoring', Campbell says.[1] There is a wasp flying very near his ear, and one of the fauns is blowing on a conch shell. Mars seems able to sleep through all of this. He may have triumphed on the battlefield, but far away from politics, love has triumphed over him, in turn.

The scene feels so eternal. Love will always triumph over war, the viewer sighs. But that is a deception. Botticelli has captured a perfect moment in time and made it eternal, but in time, it was only a moment.

Venus is not married to Mars, she is married to Vulcan, the disabled god of the forge. It was the worst coupling imaginable. They are opposites in everything that matters. She is the goddess of eroticism; he pounds iron into weapons and symbols of power. She is the essence of beauty; he is ugly. She is graceful; he has mobility issues. She attracts everyone; he attracts no one, not even his wife. She is a creature of the light, born of the sea, raised into the sky, he is a creature of cavern and cellar.

Vulcan has already summoned the other gods to witness his betrayal. While they might be chuckling up their sleeves at his cuckoldry, they give him their official support for his vengeance. Soon a giant net of fine metal – Vulcan's work – will fall on the adulterers, trapping and exposing them to the laughter of their peers.

Cupid and Psyche

In most art, Mars' and Venus' son Cupid is portrayed as a child or teenager, but one Roman poet had the imagination to let him grow up. Apuleius, the unjustly discredited author of the *Golden Ass*, conveyed a Cupid that was fully an adult.

Enter Psyche, a princess so beautiful that people travelled from far abroad to look at her. It was even whispered that she was a new Venus, but better because she was a virgin. Those who honoured the gods started offering to Psyche the kinds of adoration that, previously, they had offered Venus. Psyche received flowers, and banquets were held in her honour.

Meanwhile, and to the terrible danger of humanity, Venus' shrines were neglected. No sacrifices were made, ceremonies sacred to Venus were discontinued, her temples were even defaced in contempt. It was unendurable. It was almost as if her worshippers thought that Venus was, well, a little used up.

There is such a thing as being too pretty. Psyche would come to know that. She did not ask to be set up as a goddess. That did not stop Venus from raging at the dishonour to her altars and her following. She called her son Cupid to her side and ranted about this new human who was usurping the rights of a god.

When portrayed as a well-fed 2-year-old with a bow and arrow that can derail your life, Cupid was already dangerous enough. Apuleius' Cupid is even more frightening. In the *Golden Ass*, he is an evil homewrecker who wields not only arrows but fire.

His mother is not afraid of him, though. Venus described the problem to Cupid: a mere mortal had grasped at the worship due to none but Venus herself. The goddess commanded her son to do what only he could do: make this unworthy girl fall in love with someone ugly and stupid. Cupid agreed to help his mother.

Psyche's two sisters were beautiful in a more ordinary way, and soon they married kings. But, strangely, no proposal came for Psyche. The crowds praised her and wondered at her, but no one thought to ask for her hand. Her father suspected that, somehow, the anger of the gods was involved.

He was right, of course. The lonely Psyche, beloved of all the world for her beauty, came to hate herself. Her father sought out a priest of Apollo who told him that Psyche must be tethered to a rock and abandoned so that she could be devoured by a dragon.

Other parents might have balked at these commands, perhaps pretended not to have heard or understood them. But not Psyche's pious father who did as the oracle commanded. Psyche herself mounted no resistance. But she did reproach her parents for not behaving better. They should never have allowed the comparison to Venus. She could clearly see that the anger of the gods was behind this vicious prophecy. Weeping, her family took her to the rock and left her there.

But soon, a gentle wind swept her away and landed her unharmed in a bed of wildflowers. When she had slept, she rose and looked around. Nearby was a palace, obviously built by the gods, not humankind. The pillars were gold and there were silver and ivory appointments as well as elaborate engravings. There was so much precious metal that the house glimmered.

Disembodied voices commanded her to make herself at home, bathe, and dine. These voices assured her that they were her servants, and Psyche was not afraid of them. She perceived a divine influence in all this grandeur.

After her bath, she discovered a banquet prepared for her, again with no human, god, or creature in sight. Food and wine flew to the table, as if on a wind, and an invisible singer and harpist provided entertainment. When Psyche went to bed, her 'husband' joined her, consummated their marriage, then departed in the morning without a word. He came back on subsequent nights; eventually, he told his bride that she was in grave danger and that he was doing his best to protect her.

Meanwhile, Psyche's sisters had learned she was missing, and they were supposedly bereft and searching for her. Her new husband suspected them and told her to ignore them if she should hear their voices. But Psyche, who was lonely by day and feeling abandoned, wasted no time in asking him to bring them to her on the same wind that had brought her to this enchanted place. She wheedled, he agreed.

This invisible lord who called himself Psyche's husband also told her to give the sisters as much gold and gems as she wished. But he warned that she was not to seek to see his true form. He arrived by night and left every day before sunrise. She had no idea what he looked like, but she swore she would not attempt to see him, not even if he should turn out to be a god, which she strongly suspected. She loved him, she declared, as if he were Cupid himself. And, if you have been following the story closely, you suspect that he was.

A wind brought the sisters to Psyche, and she showed off the house and explained the voices. After the sisters had bathed and enjoyed the parade of dishes brought by invisible servers, both siblings felt a terrible surge of envy. Who was this husband? Why wasn't he around? To protect her promise to her mystery lover, she described a perfectly ordinary, fair-haired, handsome man who liked to hunt all day, then she gifted them both with gold and silver which she dropped in their laps. Psyche then commanded the wind to take them away.

The sisters found themselves on a nearby rock and, suddenly, their own perfectly good marriages to kings now seemed shabby. They had married complete strangers who used them as servants!

One sister had been wed to a bald man older than her father. The other had married an invalid, and she resented having to massage his hands with oil. The sisters intuited that Psyche had married an actual god.

They reviewed all the treasures they had seen, the gold floors, expensive robes, etc. and such fortune was totally wasted on Psyche, they agreed. Most of all, they envied their sister's happiness and worried that she would become a god as well. She was already living the life of a goddess with voices and winds for servants. Sheesh.

Soon, they had convinced themselves that Psyche had behaved arrogantly toward them, buying them off with riches, then sending them away because she was bored. Psyche should be punished, they concluded, she did not deserve her happiness.

They returned to their homes, keeping their sister's fate a secret from their parents. They hid the gifts of treasure and tore their hair to indicate they were still in mourning. Their mother and father remained unconsoled.

When he next came to her, Psyche's husband warned that her sisters were conniving against her. Specifically, he warned that these 'harlots' would convince her to unmask her husband. If she succeeded in discovering his identity, she would lose her happy home and husband, he added. He then revealed that Psyche was pregnant and promised that the child would be a god, if she obeyed her lord and husband, a mere mortal if she did not. This was happy news to Psyche who had no thought of betraying him, at that moment.

On a subsequent visit, the sisters warned Psyche that the nearby inhabitants of this region were hunting a dragon. So Psyche must be sleeping with a dragon! She must leave at once and come live with them! Poor Psyche. She mistrusted her good fortune and trusted her evil sisters, having never learned their true nature, it appears. Their warning resonated with some fear that was latent in her own mind, stemming from never having actually seen her lover.

Her sisters convinced her to take the dragon to bed and, while it was sleeping, cut off its head. They knew they had gone too far, when Psyche agreed to this, and they left as quickly as possible, breaking into a run when the wind had lifted them back up the rock. They did not even wait for their gifts.

Psyche passed a terrible day, conflicted in her thoughts, but night came finally and her husband returned to her in the dark. When he was sound asleep, she grabbed the razor with which she intended to slay him. She had hidden an oil lamp and with this light, she finally looked upon the man who called himself her groom.

He was no dragon. He was clearly a god. She could tell he was Cupid from his golden hair, perfect parts, and flawless, smooth skin. His wings were beautiful. His bow and arrows, adult weapons, lay at the foot of the bed. She examined those, too.

But she was too curious and hovered too long looking upon her beloved husband. A dollop of oil from the lamp fell on Cupid and awakened him. He saw that he had been betrayed and took off without a word, but Psyche grabbed him by the thigh. They travelled thus, he flying, she holding on until she could hold on no longer and fell to earth.

Cupid then landed above her on a cypress and started scolding. His complaints sounded a lot like the litany of complaints that husbands bring today: he had given her everything; no reasonable woman could want more than this; her sisters did not like him, and they had turned her against him; he had even defied his mother for her! How could she be so ungrateful? And a razor! Really, she was going to end him? He flew off, and she watched his departing form until it disappeared in the distance. She adored him.

In despair, she tried to drown herself in the nearest river. But rivers and trees have consciousness in the world of Roman myth. And this river knew that Psyche was Cupid's bride. Out of fear of that great god, the river refused to drown the girl, preferring to gently toss her onto its banks where a cluster of herbs provided a soft landing.

Pan was grazing his goats nearby and tutoring a young mountain goddess to sing and play the pipes. He spied Psyche and could tell she was sad for love. He spoke to her, commanding her gently not to die for love, but to pray to the love god, Cupid, humbly offering him her services. Your humble author guesses this pretty much felt to Psyche like someone rubbing salt into a cut. But she remembered her piety, made reverence to the god as she was supposed to, and departed.

In her wanderings, Psyche found herself in the city where one of her sisters lived. This sibling pretended to be delighted to see Psyche, and Psyche told her a part of her story, that she had married Cupid, unawares, and that he had abandoned her. But Psyche was less naive than she had been formerly. She told her sister that Cupid had denounced Psyche and now planned to take her sister for his wife.

No sooner had these words passed Psyche's lips than her sister took off for Cupid's palace. Standing on the now familiar rock, she prayed to be Cupid's next wife, a better one than Psyche, she vowed. Then, trusting to her fate, she jumped.

But Cupid was not listening, nor was the wind that had previously served Psyche so well. Without the help of that wind, the sister was torn apart on the rocks as she fell and soon became a meal for wild beasts. Psyche repeated this experiment with her other sister with the exact same results.

Cupid, meanwhile, was legitimately hurt from the hot oil, and he went to his mother for help. Venus flew into a rage upon learning that he had wed. She demanded to know the name of his new wife. When she learned it was Psyche, her rage accelerated. She denounced her son and threatened to clip his wings and cut his hair – both of them were gifts from her, after all, and she could take them away.

Ceres and Juno tuned into Venus' anger, and they appeared before her, demanding to know the cause of this wrath. She apprised them of the situation. Her son consorted with whores! And other women who, while not technically sex workers, were of low repute! The other goddesses attempted to reason with Venus along these lines: Your son is a love god; was he not supposed to fall in love?

Then Ceres and Juno got down to the real problem. Did Venus think Cupid was still a child? He was not, they gently noted. He was a grown man, and men fall in love and get married. Venus' sister goddesses genuinely wished to give her peace, but they were equally afraid of Cupid's arrows, so they left in a timely manner.

Meanwhile, Psyche came upon a temple into which tokens from the harvest had been carelessly thrown. The disorder offended her sense of piety, so she set about the humble task of organising the offerings. This act of devotion pleased Ceres who visited Psyche to warn her that Venus was searching for her. She praised Psyche's selflessness. Here she was, in grave danger from an angry goddess, and she was tidying a temple, heedless of her own safety.

Psyche prostrated herself before Ceres. In case you were wondering, prostrating yourself before a god involves falling to your knees, dragging your hair on the ground, and wetting the god's feet with your tears. She begged Ceres to let her hide in the temple, just for a needed rest, but Ceres' loyalty to her cousin Venus went back to a time long before Psyche's, so the goddess, regretfully, sent Psyche on her way.

In her wanderings, Psyche happened on Juno's temple. She prayed to that goddess, asking for sanctuary. As Ceres had done, Juno paid a personal visit to explain that she sympathised with Psyche. But Venus is her daughter-in-law, she said. (Your humble author would have called them half-sisters.) So Juno would not risk Venus' wrath.

Meanwhile, Venus had been searching the earth over for Psyche, to no avail. She ascended to Jupiter's rooms and demanded that he lend her Mercury to assist her. At Venus' bidding, Mercury published an announcement that whoever gave up Psyche should receive seven kisses from Venus. How quickly people forget celebrities. The same people who had abandoned the temples of Venus now hastened to betray Psyche.

Psyche finally reached the home of Venus where one of the goddess' servants recognised her. Grabbing Psyche by the hair, this servant dragged our heroine before Venus. The goddess laughed to see Psyche's distress; she ordered her servants Sadness and Sorrow to beat her, which they did. Venus then denied that any marriage between Cupid and Psyche was real; no parents had consented, and Psyche was not his equal.

Psyche was carrying a bastard with no claim on Venus' family, the goddess continued. Mocking Psyche's offer to serve, Venus assembled a pile of different grains, including wheat, barley, millet, poppy seed, beans, and lentils. She told Psyche to sort out all the grains in the heap by species, before nightfall. Then the goddess went to a banquet.

Psyche knew she could not separate out all those grains before nightfall. Remember, though, this is a world in which all the natural elements have consciousnesses and wills. A nearby queen ant had witnessed Venus' cruel behaviour, and she was outraged. She summoned ants the world over to help Psyche. They came. They sorted. By the time the sky darkened, the impossible task had been completed, and on time.

The banquet was a triumph as one suspects all Venus' occasions were. She came home quite tipsy, smelling of wine and balm, and wearing rose garlands. She took a moment to look at the grains, now carefully sorted into perfect groups. She knew Psyche had not accomplished this herself, so she assumed that Cupid had helped her.

After all, he was sequestered under the same roof, hidden from his wife and the mother of his child. Venus had already accused Psyche of hurting her son, greatly exaggerating the injury and pretending that his life was in danger. In the morning, Venus set Psyche another challenge. This time, she was to locate the golden sheep in the nearby forest and harvest some of their fur. What she did not say was that these sheep were dangerous, their foreheads were hard as rock, their horns sharp, and they were carnivorous.

Psyche rightly understood this challenge meant to get her killed, so she went to the nearest riverbank, with the intention of drowning herself, again. A sentient reed spoke up and implored her not to pollute the waters with her death. There was a way to get the wool, the reed explained.

Psyche needed to hide herself in the shade of a plane tree, behind the reeds. The sheep were most dangerous in the high afternoon heat. They would cool down in the river, then wander among some briars, leaving traces of wool in those plants. All Psyche needed to do was hide, wait, then collect the wool from the briars. Our heroine did as she was advised and took some wool home to Venus in her apron.

Venus laughed, once more, and assigned Psyche to fill a crystal bottle with the waters of the Styx and Cocytus Rivers. These rivers ran through the underworld where they functioned to separate the worlds of the living and the dead. But they had an outcropping atop a nearby mountain. Venus pointed it out and sent Psyche to fill the bottle.

Dragons guarded the rivers as they flowed down to the valley below. The flowing waters were also sentient, and their voices warned anyone within hearing that great danger was near. 'Fly, fly, or else thou wilt be slain', they said.

An eagle saw Psyche's distress. He took the bottle from her, then filled it in the rivers, dodging dragons as needed. Though the Olympians are wicked, nature and all its millions of intellects tend toward goodness. It's an idea not that different from what Wordsworth believed.

When Psyche presented the bottle to Venus, the goddess was predictably unimpressed. What would it take to get rid of the girl, might have been what she was thinking. She handed Psyche a box and told her, casually, to take it down to the underworld and ask Proserpina to give Venus some of her beauty. Venus had lost much of hers, caring for her mortally-wounded son, she explained.

Apuleuis was a shockingly modern author. Brave, strong men were rarely afforded the opportunity to see the underworld and live to talk about it. Hercules, Orpheus, Ulysses, Aeneas – whose names would resound down the centuries – these were the heroes who were brave and virtuous enough to see the afterlife, not some silly lovesick girl.

But there was a safe portal to the underworld at Mount Taenarus; it led directly to Pluto's palace where Psyche might reasonably hope to find his wife, Proserpina. But don't go with empty hands, a friendly spirit warned Psyche. Take two wet croutons, drenched in honey and barley flower. Do NOT give one to anyone who seems in need of help. Lose a crouton, you will never return to the land of the living.

Also, take two halfpenny coins, carried in your mouth. Neither the ferryman, Charon, nor Pluto, god of hell, do anything for free, the spirit noted cynically. A giant dog with three heads guards Proserpina's rooms. You must give him a crouton to get past him. On your return, you will need the second crouton to appease the dog and a second coin for

Charon. Proserpina will offer you hospitality. Sit on the ground, and ask for brown bread. Above all, do not open the box.

Psyche went down to the world of the dead, following these directions to the letter. From Proserpina, she retrieved a box of 'beauty' that Venus demanded. Having returned to the land of the living, she opened the box so she could look beautiful for her husband. The box appeared to be empty, but some magic knocked her unconscious. Apparently, Apuleuis understood that sleep is the main ingredient in beauty.

Meanwhile, Cupid had recovered from his hot oil injury. He remembered his affection for his wife, and literally flew out the window of his bedchamber. When he found Psyche, he put the 'beauty sleep' back in the box, and she awoke. He reproached her, mildly, for indulging her curiosity . . . again. But she was able to complete her assignment and take the box to Venus.

Then Cupid flew up to the heavens to petition Jupiter. Apuleius' Jupiter is much more like a judge or senator than Ovid's dangerous playboy. He summoned all the gods to a meeting and explained that Cupid had been an 'adulterous' danger to himself and others, much like a wildfire. But now, he had met a beautiful mortal woman, and this was the universe's best defence against an unwed Cupid.

In the end, it was a quick fix. Mercury flew Psyche up to heaven, and she drank from a cup that made her immortal. The wedding of Cupid and Psyche was attended by all the greater and lesser gods, including the Hours, Muses, Graces, and Pan. Apollo played on his lyre, and Venus danced.[2]

Orpheus and Eurydice

The omens were bad on Orpheus' wedding day. The groom had summoned a marriage god named Hymen to the occasion, and that god came as a guest. But there were too few joyful, smiling faces, and the wedding torches sputtered. It might have rained.

To those who read the signs, it was therefore no huge surprise when Eurydice, the bride, was suddenly dead. She had been walking through the grass with her attendants, a group of naiads, and a poisonous snake bit her. She died instantly and went to the world of the dead.

Orpheus raged through the world of the living, but to no avail. The dead do not come back. At least, they're not supposed to. But this Orpheus was no ordinary man. He was a great harpist, the son of Apollo and Calliope, who had inherited his father's godly talent. He was also a poet, a singer-songwriter, in today's parlance. Such poets sit on the fence of mortality, listening to the chatter of the gods, and putting it into song.

Orpheus found the Taenaran gateway to the underworld, This gateway was possibly in the southernmost point of Greece. This passage led him to the River Styx. From there, he moved through the shadows until he reached the thrones of Proserpina and the god Pluto.

What did that world look like? The Roman polytheistic afterlife was not the kind of life you would want. It was dark, it was shadowy. Translators of ancient Roman texts have widely agreed to use the word 'shades' to describe the residents of this afterlife. Typically, they experienced no physical pain, but they didn't have thrills either, unless they were in Elysium, a sort of heaven within the afterlife.

The underworld that Orpheus encounters is populated by many supernatural beings. A few of them were eternally tortured, but they had to seriously offend the gods to warrant punishment in the afterlife. Tantalus is one of the most famous of these offenders. He had once been a welcome dinner guest among the highest-ranking gods. But he attempted to steal nectar and ambrosia, the diet that sustained the gods' immortality, and give it to humans. Stealing food for the hungry doesn't sound like much of a crime, but if humans had eaten the food of the gods, they would have become gods themselves. And Roman gods do not like rivals or newcomers that they themselves have not vetted.

Tantalus' punishment mirrors his crime. He passes eternity in raging hunger and thirst, while standing in a pool of water over which hangs the branch of a fertile fruit tree. He can see the fruit and the water, but when he goes to take a drink, the water recedes, frustrating his effort. Similarly, the fruit is pulled just out of reach when he grasps for it.

Orpheus' underworld also contains Ixion who was tethered to a flaming wheel for crimes against the gods. Ixion was a cautionary tale of how NOT to behave in ancient Greece and Rome. He took a bride, having agreed to a bride price, then cheated his father-in-law. Later, he invited this same father to a feast and killed him by pushing him onto an open flame.

This crime put Ixion in violation of two sacred precepts – kinship and hospitality. Some scholars would say that Ixion was the first ancient Roman character to kill a relative. The Romans, who followed the Greeks in this, also held guest rites sacred. You might not be treated to a five-star meal, but, as an ancient guest, you were entitled to whatever hospitality was available. In killing a guest AND an in-law, Ixion was a savage outlier, and even the local priests would not help him absolve his crimes.

For reasons that may bypass the understanding of most scholars, Jupiter felt sorry for Ixion and invited him to dinner, at which point Ixion noticed how attractive Juno was and started hitting on her. As you can probably see, there is a pattern here.

Ordinary crimes, no matter how heinous, are not punished in the afterlife of the ancient poets. Mortal on mortal, garden-variety murder, rape, and infanticide were of no great consequence to the gods. But trifle with the gods themselves, and you will spend eternity in some hellish condition. Jupiter zapped Ixion with a lightning bolt, then commissioned Mars to build a winged wheel of fire on which Ixion would be tied forever.

Tityos, a giant, was another permanent resident of the underworld that Orpheus visited. A son of Jupiter, his story illustrates how being born with advantages doesn't always guarantee success or happiness. Even with rich and famous parents, you still have to make good choices. Tityos did not. He insulted Latona, the titan goddess who gave birth to Apollo and Diana, twin progeny of Jupiter. For this crime, he was sentenced to spend eternity stretched out over nine acres with birds tearing at his vital organs.

The story of Sisyphus, who pushes a boulder up a hill only to watch it roll back down, over and over again, throughout eternity, is probably familiar to some readers. According to Ovid, Sisyphus earned this punishment a few times over. He routinely killed his own guests. He plotted against the life of his own brother and seduced his own niece, who killed their children to keep Sisyphus from using them in his evil plans.

When he was dying, he told his wife to flout all the usual sacred funeral conventions and throw his dead body in the public square. When his soul rolled on down to the Styx, he complained to Pluto and Proserpina that his wife had disrespected him. He demanded that he should be sent back to the world of the living. Somehow, this lie worked, and he cheated death, another offence against the gods who want death to be a permanent state of affairs, on the whole. Finally, there are rumours among the Greeks that Sisyphus claimed to be cleverer than Jupiter. It's hard to imagine anybody who was asking for an eternity of pain more than Sisyphus.

The Furies also made their home in the underworld – when they were not wreaking destruction on humanity. Nominally female, the Furies are what they sound like: perpetually angry, vengeful creatures. They lived in Hades and were on call to the most powerful gods for whom they served as instruments of justice. Bestowing madness was their gift, and they could also torture and blind their victims. The Furies would descend on murderers, with special malice for those who killed a relative.

Once he was facing the king and queen of the underworld, Orpheus struck up a chord on his lyre. He sang of his love for Eurydice. In his song, Orpheus clarified that he had not descended to this realm in order to challenge death – as others had done and will do. He acknowledged the pre-eminence of death: 'yours is the longest reign that the human race must endure'.[3]

One day, both he and Eurydice would occupy this realm together, he admitted. But she had left life far too soon. In song, Orpheus begged Hades and Proserpina to 'unravel the web of my dear Eurydice's early passing'.[4] His song moved the residents of the underworld to tears.

Tantalus was so engrossed in the music that he forgot to grab at the water, Ixion's wheel stood still, and Sisyphus sat down on his boulder, the better to hear the music. The vultures who were pecking at Tityos took a break to listen, and, moved by the beauty of Orpheus' song, the Furies wept for the first and only time in their long, long lives.

The king and queen of the underworld were moved, too, and they sent for Eurydice, who limped before them – her snake bite was still fresh. They agreed that Orpheus should take his bride back to the world of the living, but with a caveat. She must walk behind him, silently, and he cannot turn around to look at her until they have ascended to the land of the living. If he does turn around, Eurydice will be retaken for the underworld, and there will be no second chance.

It sounded easy enough.

It was not easy. The passage was steep, dark, and foggy. But they ascended, slowly, with difficulty. The light of the living world broke on the horizon, but Orpheus lost faith. Did he fear that the gods had deceived him? Did he think she could have fallen behind? He could not stand another moment without seeing her. He turned.

His last look on her was brief; the forces of the underworld swept her back into the dark. He could barely hear the word 'farewell'. Bereft, Orpheus descended again to the Styx, but the ferryman pushed him away from the shore. He sat on the banks, refusing to accept his loss, refusing to eat for a week.[5]

An English poem from the Middle Ages, titled 'Sir Orfeo', retells the story, giving it a happy ending. Our hero leads his bride back to the land of the living, and they live as happily as mortals can. In Gluck's opera, *Orfeo ed Euridice*, Euridice is the one who loses faith, ascending the hill back to the living. Because Orfeo won't look at her, she believes he no longer loves her.

In the movie *Orfee*, filmmaker Jean Cocteau wrote a hero named Orpheus who falls in love with death, personified by French actress Maria Casares. He returns to his wife only because Death sacrifices herself for him. Poets, musicians, artists, anyone with creative aspirations must at least consider retelling the story of Orpheus. It's a poet's poem.

Eventually, Orpheus returned to the land of the living. He took comfort in his own songs. Upon his return to life, Orpheus positioned himself on a treeless plain and started playing on his harp and singing. Soon trees relocated themselves near to him so that they could listen. Vines followed, as well as birds and beasts. Even rocks fell in love with the sound of his voice, and they followed him. Had disappointment in love made his music even richer?

A group of savage women, dressed in deer skins, saw Orpheus singing and playing his lyre one day, in the valley below. They remembered him, specifically, as a man who would not have sex with them. These women were bacchants, i.e. followers of Bacchus, and they considered it disrespectful not to indulge pleasures of the body. One of them threw a spear at him, and another threw a rock, but these implements barely nicked him. Orpheus' music provided a barrier that physically protected him.

But the bacchants also had instruments – pipes and drums. They were not especially skilful, nor could you call the sounds they produced 'music'. Raeburn refers to it as 'cacophony'.[6] To this noise, they added clapping and shrieking, and finally they drowned out Orpheus' music.

The barrier down, they were able to attack. First they destroyed all the animals that had come to rest in his presence: birds, snakes, mammals. Then they went for the musician. They threw their staffs at him, but those implements were not meant for warfare. They threw rocks and clods of dirt, then progressed to tearing off tree branches and hitting with those.

Some farmers were ploughing with their oxen, but when they saw the bacchants, they fled. The women fell on the tools they left behind. First they killed the oxen, then Orpheus.

They tore him apart and his bones lay scattered on the meadow. The trees wept to see it. Somehow, his head and harp ended up floating down a river. The harp uttered one last plaintive note. The head sang a dirge.

The river dumped them into the ocean, and the head washed up on the Island of Lesbos. There, a snake snuck up on Orpheus' head and was about to devour it when Apollo, the great musician's patron, finally made an appearance. He turned the snake to stone and freed Orpheus' soul to descend, once more, to Hades.

He finds her, the only human he wants, on the Elysian Fields. For them, the afterlife is heaven. They walk side by side for eternity. Or sometimes Orpheus walks ahead, and Eurydice behind, but now they are sure of one another's company.[7]

PART II

THE HEROES

Chapter 4

Perseus

'Release the kraken', Sir Lawrence Olivier famously orders in the 1981 version of *Clash of the Titans*. At the time, it was difficult to imagine anyone else having the temerity to play the king of the Roman gods. But then Liam Neeson remade the part in his image in 2010. Both films, titled *Clash of the Titans*, take up the story of Perseus, the young man who killed Medusa and saved Andromeda from the sea monster, re-imagined in the last century as a close relative of Godzilla.

The Perseus story still reverberates down the ages and inspires Hollywood because it contains every element of Roman mythology that makes it timeless and riveting: arbitrary intervention of the gods; a courageous hero who is gifted with flight; multiple monsters; a femme fatale; love at first sight; a wedding; murder at the reception; and plenty of random violence.

The Perseid comes to us, fairly intact, from the ancient stories. By contrast, the story of Hercules has to be patched together from flashbacks in Seneca and slim references in Ovid, and every ancient text supports a different version. But the Perseus myth is fairly consistent across various sources, including those that cropped up in the Middle Ages and Renaissance.

Perseus' story begins with a prophecy. Acrisius, king of Argos, was ambitious, and he desired a son to carry on his legacy. He consulted a seer, and the news was not good. He would never have a son. His daughter, Danae, would give him a grandson, but this descendent was fated to kill his own grandfather – Acrisius himself.

Such prophecies were common among the ancient narratives, and they were always a test of character. If a man heard the prophecy and accepted his fate, he would at least die with dignity and at peace with the gods. Accepting the gods' will, even when it made no sense, was the ultimate piety.

But that never happened.

Instead, the men who heard this particular prophecy all committed atrocities trying to avoid the inevitable. In dodging fate, they simply became the instruments of their own destruction.

Acrisius locked his daughter in a tower (or dungeon, depending on the source) with a single servant/companion to preserve her virginity forever. Danae's happiness was of no consequence to Acrisius, only his own safety. But Danae was very beautiful, so beautiful that, even locked away, Jupiter spotted and craved her. Renaissance painters loved the story of Jupiter and Danae because the king god penetrated Danae's cloister as a cloud of golden pixie dust.[1] Painters as diverse as Titian, Orazio Gentileschi, Adolf Ulrik Wertmüller, and Andrea Casselli undertook the theme.

Front and centre of these paintings is a young, bosomy woman, the flag bearer for whatever standard of beauty prevailed at that moment in history. She is mostly or completely naked. A shower of gold dust, that sometimes looks like a rain of gold coins, falls on her, bathing her in light. A winged boy, probably a putto, accompanies her, seeming to direct traffic.

Jupiter had made love to women as a bull and swan, so nothing could stop him from making love as a rain of gold trinkets. Danae conceived the son that would, eventually, kill her father. It was a good recipe for a hero, this blending of divine power with a mortal woman. The poets are in agreement that such boys were taller, stronger, handsomer, and more radiant than other children, and they retained this aura all their lives.

For a while, Danae was able to keep the baby a secret from her father. But not forever. Perseus was a playful, joyous baby who would throw himself into his mother's arms and shower her with kisses.

Acrisius eventually heard the infant voice of his grandson, the boy predicted to bring his destruction. Crazed with fear and anger, he confronted Danae who told him, truthfully, that the child was that of Jupiter. But Acrisius denied the godly nature of his daughter's child. He wanted both his daughter and grandson dead, and only fear of the gods stopped him from murdering them on the spot. He dreaded the Furies, in particular, that species of divinity that pursued and tortured murderers, especially those who did violence against their own kin.

So Acrisius attempted a work around. He placed his daughter and grandson in an open chest and threw them in the sea. He may have had mixed feelings about doing so; Ovid is at some pains to describe the chest as an expensive one with metal trim. It was surprisingly seaworthy as well.

Danae wept to find herself so deserted, but she took comfort from knowing that her baby was too young to understand his danger. She took a moment to observe how beautiful he was, even in these perilous circumstances, and told him to sleep on his purple cloak. Then she prayed to the gods for help, modestly asking to be forgiven if anything in her prayer were too forward.

Thetis, a powerful goddess of the sea, saw Danae and her beautiful son being thrown on the waves, and she pitied them, weeping over Perseus. The goddess drove the sea chest into the nets of some fishermen, thereby saving mother and son. The chest ended up in the net of Dictis, a fisherman of Seriphos, who happened to be brother to the king of that island, Polydectes.

Dictis was unable to lift the chest himself, so he called on Silenus to help him. It would have been smarter to pray to Minerva; Silenus was notoriously unreliable, but he did show up, accompanied by other satyrs. Neither the fisherman nor the elder satyr knew what was in the chest, so they agreed to split what they hoped was treasure. When they finally fished the chest out of the water, Danae arose and explained what had happened. Her beauty, once again, would get her into the kind of trouble that no woman asks for.

Once he saw the beautiful Danae, plaything of Jupiter, Silenus wanted to marry her. Instead of approaching her honestly and directly, however, he worked Perseus, promising the boy toys and pets if he would just support Silenus' suit. He also offered to teach Perseus to hunt. These overtures met with no success, though. And soon Danae attracted the attention of Polydectes, the king of Seriphos. His intentions were not honourable either.

Danae and Perseus enjoyed a few years of peace on Seriphos. It turned out that they were distantly related to Dictis, so he took them in. Perseus continued to be a joyful child who played with lobsters in the surf. Early on, he showed a talent for working with animals. Was he a boy or man when Polydectes hatched a plot to get Perseus out of the way and rape Danae?

Perseus

Artists portray Perseus as a teenager at this stage in his career. The future killer of Medusa is tall and lean, with a super cute head of curly hair, but few or no bulging muscles. His physique is boyish, even a little feminine. His chest and face are smooth. He is conspicuously less mature than depictions of Jupiter, Apollo, and Hercules. In my mind, he is 15.

Polydectes did not propose to Danae; instead, he made a wedding contract with Hippodamia, a princess of Pisa. It was not enough to be making a good marriage with solid political connections, though. Polydectes also leveraged his engagement by demanding wedding gifts from all his subjects. Horses were the recommended donation.

Perseus was anxious to be invited to the wedding. (Clearly, he had no knowledge of Polydectes' designs on his mother.) In his innocence, Perseus asked Polydectes what kind of wedding gift he would like. Polydectes replied as he did to all his guests: he wanted another horse. He was amassing horses. That was more or less the point of getting married.

Perseus suggested, as a joke, that he would fetch the head of Medusa as a wedding present. Readers might find this problematic. Why, oh why would a boy even suggest a mission like that? Was he bragging? Was he trying to make the king laugh? Again, I find it useful to remember that he was 15. Are we really surprised that a teenager found something inappropriate to say?

Danae was a princess and, by rights, should have lived up to that standard. But she was a fugitive in Seriphos, and we must assume that she and Perseus lived a simple life, reliant on the charity of a distant relative. Somehow, though, Perseus was able to produce a horse as a gift for Hippodamia's wedding. Polydectes declined the horse, however, and demanded, instead, the head of Medusa. To Polydectes, Perseus was nothing but an obstacle to his possession of Danae. The 15-year-old needed to die and clear a path to the exiled princess.

Who was this Medusa, and why was it suicide to meet her? You probably already know that she had snakes for hair and that her gaze was deadly, turning men (and women) to stone.

But what is the rest of the story? Medusa was one of three gorgons, semi-divine offspring of a sea god. Ovid's Medusa was not a born monster. She was a beautiful young woman, originally. So beautiful that she caught Neptune's eye, and he possessed her in the temple of Minerva.

This was high treason and heresy, but the gods did not typically enact their anger on each other. That's what humans were for – to be scapegoats. Minerva, the great goddess of wisdom and defensive warfare, took her revenge on the raped maiden, and turned her into a lonely spinster with hair snakes. Medusa was doomed to be a murderer against her will, condemned to complete isolation. She was more sinned against than sinner.[2]

The very young Perseus was aghast at how swiftly and casually Polydectes had effectively ended his life, pitting him against a mortal adversary. He walked off to be alone on the opposite end of Seriphos, where people were not gifting horses and celebrating the evil Polydectes' wedding. There, Mercury visited him, inquiring why he was so sad. The magic had begun.

We have to assume that visits from the gods were rare among mortals, but not as rare for young men who were fathered by Jupiter. Ovid suggests that Mercury may have been sexually attracted to the beautiful Perseus. Technically, they were half-brothers, sired by Jupiter. Mercury, the mischief-making god and also patron of thieves, told Perseus how to find the Graiae and what to steal from them.

Armed with insight into the unseen world of demigoddesses, Perseus located the Graiae in a distant land, sometimes identified as the mythic Hesperides. They were haggard old immortals and blind, except for a single eye that they shared, passing it from one to the other and taking turns. Perseus stole this eye and also the one tooth they shared. He promised them to return these precious items if they told him where the nymphs were. Reluctantly, they did so, and he may have returned the eye and tooth or he may have wantonly thrown them in an African lake.

Next, Perseus confronted the nymphs who were gracious with gifts. From these minor goddesses, he received the winged sandals that allowed him to travel through the air, swiftly to any part of the known world. They also gave him a cap that would render him invisible and a bag that would hold the head of Medusa, rendering it harmless.

Early icons of the Perseid have him simply turning his head away from Medusa while slicing her head off with a long blade. But Ovid needed to tell a more believable story, more detailed and satisfying to the reader on an artistic level. So his Perseus observed Medusa in the reflection of his bronze shield, a gift from Minerva. With his cap of invisibility, he could see Medusa without being seen. She fell asleep and her snakes slept along with her. Using the shield to see her, Perseus killed her while she was unconscious.

The head of Medusa went in the bag donated by the nymphs. Spilt drops of her blood fell on and inseminated the ground to produce Pegasus. Pegasus, the winged horse, would enable Bellerophon to have a career parallel to that of Perseus. The blood also spawned many poisonous snakes.

The other gorgons, sisters to the murdered Medusa, pursued Perseus, but he escaped with the help of his flying sandals. So far, no artist I know of portrays Perseus flying through the heavens upside down with his shoe wings helicoptering overhead. If my first-year college physics class is not failing me, that would be a more obvious outcome of trying to fly through the air with winged feet. It's part of the magic that he remained upright.

Perseus was legitimately exhausted by this time. As he was flying through the heavens, he saw a place where it would be nice to take a break. This was the island kingdom of the Hesperides, ruled by Atlas.

Atlas and the Hesperides figure in other mythic stories, and sometimes Atlas is portrayed holding the sky on his back. The Atlas that Perseus encountered, however, seems more like a mortal king. He is a giant, but a free roaming one, up to a point, not one under a constant burden.

The Island of the Hesperides was a mythic place, the end destination of the sun god who landed his chariot there after every sunset. Atlas' kingdom was graced with an orchard of golden apples. He owned over a thousand head of livestock, but these apples were precious to him above all else, and they would be an important element in starting up the Trojan war. Atlas had built a thick wall around this orchard and even placed a dragon on the premises to guard them further. He had heard a prophecy that they would be stolen from him by the son of Jupiter.

Perseus, as soon as he touched down on this magic realm, introduced himself as the son of Jupiter, calling on Atlas to give him shelter, briefly, if he respected the gods. He claimed to be an accomplished young man – not a lie – but did not go into details. Atlas immediately assumed that this was the boy who would try to steal the apples.

Hospitality, one of the gods' absolute mandates within a system otherwise characterised by moral relativism, was withheld! Under the rules of syncretised ancient myth, Atlas was supposed to ask Perseus to stay, AND he was supposed to kill an animal, cook it, and break out the wine. Then, when both had relaxed with wine and sated their hunger, he was supposed to ask Perseus to tell his story – providing Ovid with another handy pretext for flashback. What he said instead was 'get out'.

Then he accused Perseus of lying about his origins, even though he clearly *did* believe the lad was Jupiter's son, or he would not have been so scared for his apples. Perseus replied to Atlas' rantings mildly and in a civilized manner, but he refused to leave. Atlas then tried to physically force him out. Atlas was the biggest man alive and Perseus, you might remember, was a slim, feminised teenager. I like to think that he has had a birthday since he left Seriphos. He will be married soon, and the thought of marrying at 16 makes my skin crawl just a little less.

Perseus really had no choice but to use the Medusa head on Atlas who turned into a mountain, shadowing his own carefully guarded kingdom. His head became a mountain peak, his beard and hair turned into trees, his shoulders formed a ridge. The mountain grew to such a height that the stars were able to use it as a resting place.

While Perseus was growing up on Seriphos, another beautiful teenager was coming to adulthood in distant Ethiopia. This young woman was Andromeda, and she grew up to be one of the most cherished of Roman myths, perhaps in part because she was so exotic. Some writers have insisted she was Black. Frescoes of Andromeda appear all over the remains of ancient Pompeii. They may have decorated Rome as well.

She was a princess, the daughter of the Ethiopian king Cepheus and his wife, Cassiopia. But she was not enjoying the privileged life of royalty when Perseus spied her. Cassiopia had offended the gods by claiming that she was just as pretty as the nereids. This was a blatant act of heresy, and Neptune duly punished it by sending a sea monster to ravage their coastline.

Neptune did not leave behind any clues as to how to placate the monster, so Cepheus consulted a priest, as the ancients did when all else failed. The priest, Ammon, told him that he must sacrifice Andromeda to the monster. Nothing else would erase the blasphemy Cassiopia had done.

So Cepheus reluctantly had Andromeda chained to a rock, her arms spread out at her sides and pinned down, her feet pinned to a rock.

The Roman poet, Marcus Manilius, verbally paints her waiting for the monster's attack as if she were waiting for her bridegroom on her wedding night. Manilius even puts her in something like a wedding dress, though this slips, leaving her partially naked. The poet briefly notices her snow-white neck and how the rocks on which she is chained contrast with her soft skin and limbs. Manilius even describes her as a martyr on her 'virgin cross'.[3]

Alternatively, artists and poets portray Andromeda as chained up just at the front of a cave; the cave mouth functions to frame her as a statue in an alcove, perhaps on the outside of a temple. Either way, she was intensely sexy. So much so that Perseus almost forgot to keep his sandal wings flapping when he saw her. She looked like a marble statue, except that he could see her long hair blowing in the wind, and tears coursed down her beautiful cheeks.

His first words to Andromeda declared his intention to love her. She should not be bound like this, in a criminal's chains. Instead, he declared, she should be bound by the love of a man. Andromeda was too lady-like to talk to a man directly and without a chaperone, so she cried some more.

But then it occurred to her that, if she did not speak up in her own defence, this gentleman would conclude that she was a felon of some kind. So she told her story – how her mother had brought the fury of the gods down on Ethiopia. She didn't have time to tell him about the monster, because while they were talking, that beast broke though the waves, covering most of the view with its massive chest.

Who and what was this monster? Ogden refers to it as a ketos, the Greek word for 'sea monster'. 'Cetus' was the Roman equivalent. Some translators want it to be a dragon. And for some inexplicable reason, movie makers think it's a kraken, possibly because a full-grown, deep-sea cephalopod is something you could never, realistically, expect to see at the surface of the ocean. By the time a real-life giant squid drifts to the top of the ocean, it is well dead or dying, of old age and intolerable water pressure.

When love at first sight is so definitive, a marriage proposal must follow afoot. Conveniently, Andromeda's mother and father were nearby, watching and waiting for their daughter to be gruesomely torn apart. Perseus approached them and bargained to save Andromeda if he could wed her. He quickly recited his resume – son of Jupiter, killer of

Medusa – and explained that he would now add to his list of amazing accomplishments by defeating this dragon.

Andromeda's parents quickly agreed and sweetened the deal with a kingdom. Clearly Cassiopia and Cepheus were in no position to negotiate. An older man, one not so beautiful or obviously the son of a god, would probably have been accepted into the family at this point in time.

Not a moment too soon, for the dragon was near. The water's surface parted for him as it would for the bow of a ship. Soon, it was as close to the reef where Andromeda was chained. Perseus leapt into the sky, aided of course, by wings, and cast a shadow on the dragon, which distracted the creature. Perseus plummeted and stabbed the beast with his curved blade.

He attacked the creature's flank, back, even the thinning part of its tail. The stricken monster reared into the sky and then dove, trying to escape the pain. It vomited brine and purple blood. Perseus' winged sandals were waterlogged by the foaming sea. He could no longer fly, so he took his stand on a barely visible jetty. From that position, he finally delivered four death blows to the dragon's guts.

The humans rejoiced at the monster's defeat, and they were joined by the gods in heaven. Curiously, Perseus immediately took time to care for the head of dead Medusa, laying her gently face down in some seaweed. Medusa's glare turned the seaweed hard, and the nearby sea goddesses distributed the hardened weeds, creating coral reefs near coastlines everywhere. Ovid was not a scientist, but he did understand nature's processes better than most. A quick google search shows that coral is partly seaweed as well as algae and phytoplankton.

Perseus was a devout young man, and he knew that his sacrifices to the gods, in gratitude for his victory, must take place promptly. He built three altars, the centremost was for Jupiter, on which Perseus sacrificed a bull. Flanking that were altars to Mercury and Minerva. To Mercury, his half-brother, he sacrificed a calf, and to Minerva a cow.

He wed Andromeda quickly after that. He asked for no dowry. Music accompanied the wedding celebrations. There was song and the music of lyres and flute. Neighbours garlanded their roofs with wreaths. Incense burned throughout the kingdom.

Cepheus pulled out all the stops on the wedding, inviting his neighbours to a huge banquet. This event was interrupted with a terrible clamour when Phineas angrily stormed the wedding party. To understand what happened next, we must remember that close familial relationships in marriage were not eschewed by the Romans as much as they are by contemporary western society. Cousins could marry. This liberalism applied to uncles and nieces as well.

Phineas was the king's brother, and he had been betrothed to Andromeda before she was tethered to the rock. Phineas had already heard of Perseus' accomplishments; he crashed the party yelling at Perseus that no winged sandals or shower of gold would save him now.

Cepheus attempted to reason with his brother. Perseus didn't rob him of Andromeda; that was the nereids and Ammon, he noted. He also pointed out the rules that surround treatment of guests. Finally, he pointed out that Phineas had seen Andromeda, with his own eyes, get chained to a rock.

Phineas had done nothing. He had not raised an army; he hadn't attempted to kill the sea monster. Cepheus didn't choose between Perseus and Phineas. He chose between Perseus and the death of his daughter. Phineas had relinquished his claim, his brother concluded.

None of this logic prevailed on Phineas. He launched a spear at Perseus, but it went wide of the mark and got embedded in a couch. Perseus was quick to pull it out of there and thrust it at Phineus who took shelter behind an altar. Rhoetus, a wedding guest with no dog in this fight, took the full force of the spear in his face. As he was dying, his blood stained the wedding table. It was the start of war.

The assembled guests very quickly turned into a crazed mob. They called for the deaths of Perseus and Cepheus. Cepheus had fled the building, however, calling out to the gods to witness that he had tried to avert this savagery.

Minerva sped to the scene. She did not end the conflict, as she could have done. Instead, she shielded Perseus as the combat continued. Any son of Jupiter was Minerva's full sibling, but it is worth noting that the gods often held back their intervention until the hero had shown audacity. A quip that many believers use applies here with only slight modification: 'Gods help those who help themselves'.

The battle cry of the wedding guests was 'Kill Perseus', so he lashed out at everyone with little to no discrimination. One of his first victims was a teenager named Athis. He was a lovely, androgynous boy from

India. He was lavishly dressed in purple and gold, bejewelled, with a gold circlet holding his myrrh-scented hair. He was the beloved friend, or perhaps the lover, of Lycabas, another teenager. Ovid uses a word that translates as 'love', but who knows what he meant by that?[4]

Athis was skilled in bow and javelin, but he got no chance to show off those skills because Perseus grabbed a burning log from the altar and smashed Athis' face to fragments. Lycabas wept to see the life bleed out of his friend, and he picked up Athis' bow and arrows, preparing to fight Perseus. Lycabas' arrow lodged in Perseus' tunic, but missed his body. Perseus chopped at the boy with his curved blade, and Lycabas died swiftly, but not before he had positioned himself to fall beside Athis. The two of them journeyed to the underworld together.

Perseus did not have a second to rest. Phorbus and Amphimedon were eager to join the fray, but they slipped in the blood already spilled on the floor, and Perseus took advantage of their distraction by stabbing them in the ribs and throat. Erytus was skilled in axe combat, but as he readied for the fight, Perseus coshed him with a giant mixing bowl. The blow broke open his head and killed him.

One banqueter, Idas, would have done better to flee the palace with the king. He avoided the fighting, refusing to take a side. But Phineas again launched a spear at Perseus. It missed, again, but hit this Idas. Heroically, he tried to pull the weapon from his body and use it against Phineas. But as soon as he had pulled the shaft out of himself, he discovered the wound was mortal. He died without another word.

Emathion, a debilitated old man with a strong sense of justice, should have stayed out of the way. He was far too old to fight. Proving that age does not necessarily bestow wisdom, this Emathion thought he could talk the mob down. They had no use for his advice. He clung to the altar for sanctuary and uttered a string of curses. When Chromis beheaded him, Emathion's head flew into the air and landed, upright, on the altar where it continued cursing for an appalling amount of time. Finally, his tongue grew thick and still over the open flame.

The bodies were falling so hard that, at one point, Perseus took his stand on a pile of them. Phineus kept killing innocents. He took down Broteas and Ammon, brothers who had excelled at boxing but not swordplay. He also killed a priest of Ceres.

The lute player was not even a guest at this party cum war. He was only there because he'd been hired to sing and play for the banquet. This Lampetides, by name, stood weapon-less in the midst of the impromptu battle. In one hand, he still held the quill he used to pluck the strings of his instrument. Possibly he kept singing, if only from habit.

By rights, he should not have been targeted. But a guest named Pettalus had no real sense of fair play. 'Sing that song in hell!' he yelled as he struck and killed the bard with a blow to the forehead. As he fell, the musician struggled to play a last chord on his instrument.

The combatants had come for a party, so there was a shortage of actual weapons. The fighters found ways to use what was at hand. One Lycormas witnessed the murder of the lute player and sought to avenge him. To that end, he tore an iron bar off the door and broke Pettalus' neck as a butcher slaughters a bull.

Inspired by Lycormas, Pelates tried to pull another bar from the door, but as he was reaching, a blade pierced his hand and then Abas killed him with a mortal thrust. Morbidly, the dead man did not fall. He stayed upright, held in place by the spear in his hand.

Halcyoneus killed Dorylas with a spear to the groin. Dorylas was a man of wealth; in killing him, Halcyoneus mocked him for acquiring new acres, presumably in the underworld. Still under the protection of Minerva, Perseus avenged Dorylas with Halcyoneus' spear which he pulled from the corpse. The tip was still warm with Dorylas' blood as he drove the spear into Halcyoneus' nose and neck. In the next moment, he killed twins who fell together. One he skewered in the thighs; the other took a spear to the mouth.

By this time, the few men siding with Perseus were all dead, his father-in-law flown, and the screams of his bride and mother-in-law could not be heard over the clash of arms and the vocalisations of dying men. The household gods were polluted by the blood of the murdered.

Soon, the mob formed a circle of a thousand men, and they surrounded Perseus. The arrows they rained on him were thick as a hailstorm. Perseus put his back up against a pillar, to guard his rear. He wounded Molpus, but that man escaped because there was only one Perseus and a thousand enemy fighters. Perseus was saved from death only because a blow went awry and hit the pillar. A chunk of the pillar broke free and flew into the throat of another man. Perseus finished him with his scimitar.

Finally, Perseus admitted to himself that this crowd was too big to vanquish, so he gave them all a last chance. 'If anyone considers me a friend, turn your back to me now', is a loose translation of what he shouted. There were no friends, but the combatants didn't take him seriously. 'Find someone else to scare with your riddles', Thescelus cried and pulled back his javelin for the killing blow.

Before he could launch his weapon, his arm started turning to stone. Perseus had exposed the Medusa head to the assembled fighters. Moments later, a few threats lingered in the air, but half the fighters had been turned to statues, most of them with weapons poised to kill.

How did Phineas, of all people, survive the Medusa head? I can only assume that the former fiancé of Andromeda anticipated the Medusa move and turned away, as did some others. With his face pointed away from Perseus, he started wildly bargaining for his life. He didn't hate Perseus, he was quick to explain. Nor did he have political ambitions. He was just fighting for his fiancée. Perseus had the better claim to Andromeda; he could see that clearly now. He asked only for his life to be spared.

Perseus saw no reason to pardon this man who had caused the needless death of so many good people. He would not put Phineas to the sword, he declared. Instead, Phineas would become a memorial of sorts – a statue in the home of Perseus' father-in-law. Then he walked the Medusa head over to where Phineas was standing and petrified him. The tears running down his face turned to stone. His hands, clenched in begging, and his craven posture were frozen, marking him a coward for all time.

Perseus left Ethiopia immediately. After all, he had winged sandals. Taking his bride into his arms, he flew off with her. He did not take her to Seriphos. Instead, he went to his fatherland, Argos.

The face of that kingdom had changed radically since Danae's expulsion. Acrisius' brother, Proetus, had successfully overthrown Acrisius and declared himself king of the realm. The two had been hated rivals most of their lives, and now Proetus was ruling Argos from a fortress. Perseus dispatched him with little ceremony, using the Medusa head. Then he restored the kingdom to his vicious grandfather.

Does this mean that Acrisius escaped his fate and was never killed by his grandson? Of course not. But that prophecy took a long time to come true.

Perseus

At some point, Perseus had cause to return to Seriphos where he and Danae had taken refuge so many years earlier. Polydectes' hatred of Perseus was still so intense that he dismissed our hero's deeds as fiction. Perseus produced the proof, the head of Medusa herself, warning the people assembled to avert their eyes. Polydectes, however, was looking right at him, and the head turned him to stone in a few seconds.

By all accounts, Perseus' marriage to Andromeda was a happy, productive one. They had at least seven children and many descendants, among whom was Hercules.

There is a rare fresco in Pompeii that portrays Perseus and Andromeda sitting peacefully by a pool of water in which they can see Medusa's lethal head reflected. Perhaps they are both meditating on how miraculous it is that they are alive. The gods saved Perseus, and he saved his wife. The couple might be sending up silent prayers of gratitude.

'Perseus is an easy hero to admire, but a hard one to like', writes Daniel Ogden. 'Of all the major Greek [and Roman] heroes, he is the only one to whom it is difficult to attribute a personality'.[5] He goes on to note that Perseus has none of the moral failings that evoke character; he doesn't throw his own child and grandson into the surf, hoping they'll just die, he doesn't kill his wife in a mad rage, he doesn't sacrifice one of his own children for a good sailing wind.

Perhaps we have confused public drama with personality. You have a good chance of staying out of the tabloids if you can just stop acting out. In fact, Perseus' post-Ethiopia life resembles that of many good men who remain un-derailed by bad choices.

As a grown man, Perseus is credited with founding Mycenae, and here we find the hero reaching across the chasm of literature to appear in the historical record. More than one monument to Perseus has been found in the ruins of Mycenae, rediscovered in 1700 AD by a Venetian engineer. In ancient times, Mycenae was an important military stronghold, with a fortress and, at its height, about 30,000 residents.

Beyond that, we might have to assess Perseus' personality from the kind of trouble he did not get into. Despite Acrisius' attempt to kill Perseus and Danae, Perseus never exacted revenge on his biological grandfather. In fact, he served Acrisius fiercely.

In this, he conformed to an ancient ideal. One does not kill one's father or other male ancestor under any circumstances, even when he richly deserves it. The Greeks and perhaps the Romans had a convenient belief that the baby is transferred from the male body to the female body intact, with no participation of the woman. She provides no egg, he provides all the material. In other words, a woman merely incubated the baby until its birth. This erroneous natural history made the life of a father far more precious than the life of a mother.

Many heroes would not be so loyal to a murderous grandfather, but Perseus was pious in a way especially valued by the ancients. So, when Acrisius died by Perseus' hand, it was a bizarre accident. It took place, not on the battlefield, but on the field of friendly competition.

The ancients did love their sports. One of Perseus' greatest accomplishments was to invent the quoit. Quoits, in which the object of the game is to throw a rope or metal ring on or near a goalpost of some kind, is still played in the United Kingdom today as a traditional sport. To the non-athlete, or the random American, it might look quite a lot like horseshoes. One must assume that the quoits invented by Perseus had to have been iron, not rope, because of what happened when they were test driven.

In Larissa, a Greek city which still thrives today, the king staged an athletic competition, and would-be heroes came from all over to prove themselves fit for adventure and heroism. Perseus was there to introduce his game of quoits. He may or may not have known that Acrisius was there. Either way, Perseus threw a quoit and it hit Acrisius by accident. Let us hope Acrisius was killed instantly and did not die of slow sepsis from a minor injury, as one source cruelly has it.

In either event, using ancient Roman ethical standards, Perseus is guiltless of his grandfather's death. Acrisius is also saved – from an ignominious legacy that re-emphasises just what an infanticidal lunatic he is. The final result of Perseus' decency and piety is that the old man has a few more good years before dying on a field of sorts – 'a good death', the gods would chuckle.

Sir Walter Scott, that Scottish all around poet/novelist/historian, ventured to write a long poem about Perseus in the nineteenth century. Scott gives Acrisius a quick death, but doesn't shed many tears about it. So this ending might more or less resonate with the reader's feelings:

Perchance it is the wind or fate
That bears adverse the bounding quoit,
Thus hurled in sport beyond the rest,
And sinks into his grandsire's breast.
So dies the king; alas! who knew?
Acrisius dies; the gods are true.[6]

You might now be saying to yourself, 'But, but, Clash of the Titans! He rides Pegasus, the winged horse!' Yes, winged sandals seem lame in comparison to a horse that flies. But the ancients were unanimous on this point: winged sandals, possibly the gift of a very bisexual Mercury. I myself had always assumed that Hollywood was solely and wholly to blame for putting Perseus and Pegasus in the same story. But Ogden traced the problem back down the centuries, through the Renaissance to the high Middle Ages and found that Boccaccio's wonderful, erotic, satiric, bawdy *Decameron* was among the first texts to put Perseus on that steed.

It is easy to see how, a few hundred years down the line, a poet or artist might confuse Perseus with Bellerophon, the ancient rider of Pegasus. Pegasus is, after all, born as a footnote to the Perseus story. Blood from the slain Medusa germinates to give life to this beautiful creature. Minerva favoured Bellerophon as she did Perseus, and with the goddess' help, he rose to greatness by slaying the Chimera monster. Bellerophon was more Greek hero than Roman, so I will gently set him down here, and you can read more in Euripides, if you care to.

The flying horse was virtually irresistible to artists and writers of the Middle Ages and Renaissance. The myths of Perseus and Bellerophon, as they merged, made themselves useful to Christian artists, who used some of that imagery, notably the armour, shield, and weaponry, to feature Saint George killing a dragon. Knights became the warriors of Christ in the crusades, and knights needed horses. Therefore, it is unlikely that Perseus, who became the model of a British knight, would ever trade his magic horse back in for sandals.

Chapter 5

Hercules

When you opened this book and read the word 'Hercules', a picture formed in your brain, probably. An alpha male, broad shouldered, muscle bound, tall, perhaps he is picking up a giant boulder.

That stereotype IS Hercules, but he was more than that. He was originally a Greek and Phoenician hero, going roughly by the name 'Herakles', among the Greeks and 'Melquart' among Phoenicians and their colonists. The Romans latched on to him, and hard.

That's because Hercules, as they renamed him, was the ideal Roman man: strong, courageous, good-natured, good-humoured, respectful of the gods, a tireless lover, and a loving husband and father – most of the time. He was both blessed and cursed by fate and the gods, and his ability to rise above the tragedies of his life defines him more than his great strength.

Hercules was conceived and born into a whirlwind of drama. His mother, Alcmene, had married Amphitryon, a mortal man of great skill and strength, and a grandson of Perseus. But they had not consummated the marriage.

Alcmene's brothers had been murdered during her engagement, and she assigned her husband to avenge their deaths. She would not sleep with him until it was done. An unavenged death was a terrible dishonour.

Jupiter followed Amphitryon as the latter set out to avenge his wife's brothers. Then, when Amphitryon had succeeded in executing the killers, Jupiter disguised himself perfectly as Amphitryon, fresh from battle, and entered Alcmene's bedroom. He recounted the execution of her brother's murderers with convincing detail; after all, he had been watching. Alcmene took him into her arms and gave Jupiter all the passion she had been saving for her lawfully-wedded husband.

To get the most mileage out of his stolen hook up with Alcmene, Jupiter made that one night last three days. There were a lot of moving parts to this break. The sun had to park his chariot and keep his horses calm. The moon also had to cooperate and move in slow motion for three days.

Nosy humans were put to sleep for about seventy-two hours, so they didn't notice that night was lasting far too long. Even rosy-fingered Dawn kept her hands out of the sky while Jupiter and Alcmene celebrated what she thought was her wedding night. Upon leaving her bedside in the morning, Jupiter congratulated himself that he had sired a boy who would surely be a great hero.

Then he returned to Olympos and his wife, Juno. He did not betray his lover deliberately. But he was given to bragging, and he could not stop himself from indulging some locker room banter with the other male gods. Juno was nearby, listening to every word. No child of Jupiter was safe, if born to a mortal woman. Juno stalked Hercules through his entire life, forever scheming to bring him misery. He lasted longer than anyone could reasonably have predicted, but she destroyed him in the end, ensuring that Jupiter would respond by granting his bastard son immortality.

When the blind seer Tiresias explained to Amphitryon that his wife had conceived with Jupiter, no harm came to Alcmene. If the gods want something from the mortal world, there is no point arguing. To do so could even be construed as heresy. Alcmene learned of the deception from her husband and spent some time musing on why a god would consider her worthy of such a gift.

Alcmene gave birth to two sons after her night with Jupiter. Hercules' fraternal twin, Iphicles, was Amphitryon's son, conceived on the night after Hercules had been sired. Their mother feared for both of them, but she could not bear for Iphicles to become collateral damage in Juno's inevitable revenge. So she abandoned Hercules in a meadow, thinking that Juno could kill him without hurting the rest of the family.

But Jupiter had an eagle that spied for him, much like a drone. This eagle spotted the abandoned child and reported the matter to his king. Jupiter then enlisted Minerva to help him effectively prank his wife. Minerva asked Juno to accompany her on a walk, and the two 'happened upon' the baby Hercules. 'What a beautiful specimen of humanity. Why would anyone abandon such a strong, healthy baby boy?' was approximately what Minerva wondered out loud. 'Juno, you have breasts. You should nurse him.'

The queen of heaven took the boy to her breast and nursed him, but soon he clamped down way too hard. The goddess of marriage and motherhood was quick to throw that baby off her chest. In the process, she and Hercules created the milky way of constellations. Her breast milk splattered across the sky turning into those stars.

That bite opened Juno's eyes to the deception. She stormed off, freshly outraged that she had just fed her enemy. She would now plan her revenge. The small amount of Juno's milk that Hercules drank gave him godlike strength for a lifetime.

Amused, Minerva disguised herself as a nondescript country lass, picked up the baby, and carried him back to Athens and his mother. Alcmene had been brooding on the ethics of her decision and, more importantly, how she was going to explain Hercules' absence to her husband. Then, this stranger appeared with her baby.

As happened sometimes, the light of Minerva's divinity flashed from under the hem of her gown, giving away her true identity. From that, Alcmene knew this was a visit from the gods. She fell to her knees and bowed before Minerva. Minerva gayly told the new mother to raise her son well and vanished.

Juno was by no means done trying to kill Hercules in his infancy. When he and his human twin were a few months old, she sent two giant blue snakes to kill the babies. They slithered across marble floors to the bed in which Alcmene had laid the children for the night.

As one of the snakes reared to strike, Iphicles woke, screamed and tossed off his blanket. By the time Amphitryon had arrived with men and weapons, the monsters were dead and in a heap. Hercules had strangled both snakes with his tiny hands.

As a child, Hercules had the kind of education that most of us only dream of. The great Castor, hero of the Argonauts and the Trojan War, taught the boy to fight. He learned to drive a chariot, shoot bows and arrows, sing, and play the lyre. Eventually the wise and learned centaur, Chiron, became his lead tutor.

The centaurs were a race of horses with human heads and torsos. Chiron was not born into the race of centaurs, however. He was the son of Saturn, the ancient titan who sired Jupiter. Saturn took the form of a horse one day and raped a nymph who became Chiron's mother.

With immortals on both sides of his parentage, Chiron could not die, though he did develop grey hair and a grey beard in time. He associated with centaurs, but he did not share in their impulsive, often violent natures. Chiron was legendary as a teacher, and he went on to tutor the great Greek fighter Achilles after Hercules grew up.

To the dismay of Chiron and his parents, Hercules betrayed an anger problem early in childhood. His lyre teacher, Linus, hit him for playing a bad note, and Hercules responded by hitting his teacher back, with the lyre, and killing him instantly.

He stood trial and defended himself eloquently, mounting a sort of 'stand your ground' argument, and he was exonerated. That was the end of Hercules' formal education, however. Amphitryon, still worried about his stepson's temper, sent him to a remote mountain to herd cattle and learn, if possible, inner peace.

Hercules remained in the mountains until he was a young adult, and it was there that he faced his famous 'crossroads'. One day, the goddesses of vice (also known as pleasure) and virtue (also known as duty) approached him from across a meadow. Vice, gaily dressed in loud colours and jewellery, offered him a lifetime of joy, wine, parties, and little hardship, if he would be her follower.

Instead, Hercules dedicated his life to Virtue, who was very demure and dressed modestly all in white with no adornments. The path of virtue is hard, she admitted, and he would have to control his passions. He chose that hard, narrow path. By implication, he committed himself to curbing his violent streak. He would not always be successful.

Sometime later, Hercules and his stepfather, Amphitryon, were caught up in an armed conflict between the Thebans and the Minyans who were enforcing a cruel annual tribute of cattle on Thebes. Hercules won the day against the Minyans. In gratitude, King Creon gave him Megara, the king's eldest daughter, as a wife. To Hercules' brother, Iphicles, Creon gave another of his daughters.

Hercules and Megara went to live with his mother Alcmene, and the hero settled down to a happy married life. He was enchanted with his new bride. Over the next few years, she bore him at least two sons. Iphicles lived nearby and his children grew up with those of Hercules. Iphicles' son, Iolaus, would be one of Hercules' most legendary companions.

Hercules had everything a reasonable man could wish for: a beautiful wife, children, happy siblings, a living mother, height, strength, and the great admiration of his people. Even before he had undertaken the labours and the adventure of the golden fleece, his contentment was enough to stoke Juno's rage at an affair that happened over twenty years earlier.

The Myceanean king, Eurystheus, had been Juno's agent all his life. Juno had intervened in his destiny before he was even born when she forced him into his mother's birth canal prematurely, to ensure he was born before his cousin Hercules. This gave Eurystheus a better claim to the throne of Tiryns than his stronger, braver relative.

Juno protected Eurystheus, but Hercules was the darling of many other gods, especially Jupiter and Minerva. When he began his labours, Hercules was divinely armed with the bow and arrows of Apollo, a helmet from Minerva, a sword from Mercury, a horse from Neptune, and a shield from Jupiter. The gods that did not yet love Hercules would be won over by him, as he established himself as the world's strongest, most resilient, most clever champion.

Twelve Labours

As Juno's agent and king, Eurystheus became Hercules' taskmaster. He was exactly the kind of man for whom Hercules had nothing but contempt. Eurystheus stayed safe within his city walls while others struck out for adventure. He was prone to jealousy and petty revenge.

The fact that the two men were cousins invited comparisons between Hercules' intrepidness and Eurystheus' caution. Starting out, Eurystheus identified actual threats to humanity that needed to be addressed. Later on, it was obvious that he felt threatened by Hercules and was attempting to get him killed.

Hercules was first tasked with killing the Nemean lion, a magical beast fathered by a two-headed dog. At least one poet believed that the lion had been raised by Juno and was under her protection. Its fur was impenetrable. No one knew the exact location of the lion, so Hercules travelled the ancient Peloponnese, the southern peninsula of today's Greece, searching. Shepherds and their families pointed the way.

When he located the beast, Hercules quickly learned that his arrows glanced off it without harming him. He drove the animal to its cave, blocked off the back exit, then entered the cave from its mouth, ready to fight to the death. A blow from Hercules' giant club gave the creature pause, but in the end, he had to strangle the lion as he had the snakes.

What glory is there for the lion killer if he does not wear the fur of his foe as a signifier of his courage and strength? Hercules set about skinning the lion, but quickly learned that ordinary tools would not budge that fur. Minerva saw him struggling and informed him that the only tool sharp enough to cut that skin was the lion's own claw.

He wore the lion skin from that time forward, and it frequently saved his life as it could not be pierced or cut. As Juno mourns in *Hercules Furens*, every time she tries to kill him, he just gets more famous. He wears the souvenirs of his triumphs – the club and lion skin – and they form a brand.[1]

He re-entered the kingdom of Eurystheus bearing the dead lion wrapped around his shoulders. The king was both impressed and terrified. He directed Hercules not to bring any more dead animals inside the city walls. In fact, Hercules should stay out of the city altogether and just display his trophies to the wall guards, the king declared.

The Hydra

Then Eurystheus set Hercules the task of killing the Lernaean hydra, a monstrous snake with multiple, regenerating heads and poisonous breath. Juno had, herself, nurtured this magical creature specifically to kill Hercules. The hydra's breath was so toxic that she could kill people while she was sleeping, if they got too close.[2] By the time the Roman poets got around to imagining the hydra, she grew two or three heads back every time Hercules chopped one off.[3]

Approaching the hydra, Hercules covered his nose and mouth with cloth to prevent himself from being poisoned, then he shot some arrows. These failed, as they had with the lion. Next, he tried clubbing the snake and cutting its heads off with a harvesting scythe. But the heads grew back and multiplied.

Stumped, Hercules called on his nephew, Iolaus, for help. With Minerva's help, the two hatched a plan wherein Hercules cut off a head and Iolaus cauterized the bloody neck stump with a torch, preventing regeneration. This plan worked, but, as always, Juno was watching.

In a move typical of 1970s special effects cinematographers, Juno sent in a giant crab to give Hercules something else to do besides defeat the monster at hand. Hercules crushed the crab with his foot and then turned his attention back to the snake.

The hydra, he soon learned, had one immortal head. Here, again, Minerva assisted, lending Hercules her own sword to finally end the beast. Appalled, Juno turned her dead pet into the Hydra constellation which burns in the sky today. The crab she turned into the Cancer constellation. Hercules took the precaution of dipping his arrows in toxic hydra blood, and he would use those embellished weapons later.

The Giant Deer and the Erymanthian Boar

Hercules' next labour was to capture a giant female deer, often referred to as the Ceryneian hind, named after its habitat. The beast was interfering with wine production by chasing farmers away from their own vineyards. It was larger than a bull and had golden hooves and a brindled hide. Even with giant golden antlers, this creature was clearly the least menacing animal Hercules had been sent to subdue. Where were her claws of steel, her murdering gaze, her poisonous breath?

Deer, in general, were under the protection of Diana, goddess of the hunt and a committed forest dweller. This deer that Hercules was to subdue was especially sacred. Diana had discovered a herd of five such hinds, and she prized them. Four of them she tamed and harnessed to pull her chariot, but she left the fifth one wild, possibly foreseeing that Hercules would need to capture it one day.

There is a divergence among the ancient writers about whether Hercules killed, injured, or captured the magic deer. In one version of the story, he simply breaks off one of the animal's antlers in the presence of Apollo and Diana, who permit him to violate a sacred deer in this way because he is Hercules.

The next task was to capture and transport the Erymanthian boar, a huge wild pig, foaming at the mouth, and terrorising a set of glens and marshes. Hercules found it, gave chase, wounded it, and drove it into a snowbank where he was able to chain the beast. He then threw it over his shoulder, fettered but alive, and took it back to Mycenae where he threw it down in the public meeting place, very much against Eurystheus' instructions.

That king appears to have been born anew every morning. Again, he was surprised that Hercules survived the task and also frightened of the demi-god's growing popularity and fame. After seeing Hercules carrying the boar, its blood drying on the back of his shirt, he had a giant bronze panic room built for himself.

Ancient poets refer to the panic room as a 'vessel' or a 'jar'. It became the king's custom to hide himself in it, especially when Hercules was back in town with a dead monster to display. He did summon the courage to keep handing out labours. But, for safety, he sent staff members out to negotiate with the hero and give him his marching orders.

Around this time, Hercules found himself near Mount Pelion where he ran into an old friend, the centaur Pholus. Like his former tutor, Chiron, Pholus was an enlightened centaur, not one of the rowdy, impulsive, and dangerous band of regular centaurs. The centaurs ate a raw food diet, but Pholus remembered his manners and invited Hercules to dine on something more palatable.

Hercules asked for wine which aroused all kinds of anxiety in his host. When it came to drinking, the centaurs were much better off leaving the stopper in the flagon. They were not gracious in inebriation, and they were known to pick quarrels. Even the smell of booze could get them on their feet, spoiling for a fight. As a result, they had basically agreed not to drink individually. When they drank, they drank together, and everyone shared.

Pholus, who wore the unenviable mantle of role model to this band of carousers, did not want to open a bottle of wine anywhere near the other centaurs. And they were nearby. He also remembered that, long ago, Bacchus had left a jar of wine with the centaurs. It was meant for a special occasion.

Out of piety, they had never decanted this jar. There had not been an occasion special enough. But now there was. Hercules' reputation had travelled over the entire civilized world. It was either known or intuited that he had godly powers and a godly genealogy.

Pholus concluded that this was the occasion on which to open the wine. But to avoid the gaze, and possible censure, of the centaurs, they retired to a cave to drink. What they had not counted on was how strong and fragrant the wine would be.

The smell drifted to the keen noses of the other centaurs. They arrived at the cave mouth prepared to do murder over unshared alcohol. They tore trees out of the ground to use as clubs. But these clubs could not save them from Hercules' poisoned arrows. A mere nick was enough to kill man or beast.

The conflict occurred at night, and Hercules could not tell one centaur from another. Before long, there was a heap of dead bodies just outside the cave. And more centaurs were coming to the aid of their tribe, their angry hoofbeats clamouring through the mountains.

Hercules started picking them off at a distance, and at the tail end of the unequal battle an arrow ricocheted and hit Chiron in the leg. It was not a mortal wound, but the hydra poison brought Hercules' old tutor excruciating pain. And he could not die, because of his immortal parents.

Pholus had wisely stayed behind in the cave while Hercules dispatched the mad centaurs. Now he came forth, and took stock of the amassed carnage, observing that some centaurs were dead who had only superficial wounds. He was fascinated with the poisoned arrows and removed one from a comrade to study it. It slipped out of his hand and landed on his foot, point first, killing him instantly.

The Augean Stables and Stymphalian Birds

Hercules kept surviving impossible tasks, and his fame was growing. People respected him more than they respected their own kings. The next labour was designed, therefore, to humble him.

Our hero was charged with cleaning out the Augean stables which housed 3000 cattle, the most of any family in Greece of that time. The cattle were immortal, while also in possession of healthy lower intestines. No courageous soul had even tried to clean their stables.

Ordinary livestock would have died of disease and infection if their stable were that nasty. But these cattle were immune to the ravages of E. coli that plague lesser mammals. They were the private property of Augeas, the king of Elis, a Greek city-state.

The intent of the assignment was to give Hercules something grubby to do. This was the work of an unloved janitor. The image of Hercules carrying a giant bloodied animal on his back or shoulders had burned itself into the imagination of way too many people. He would not on this occasion, Eurystheus hoped, distinguish himself that way.

Augeas himself was no particular friend of Hercules, but he did offer to reward the labourer with one tenth of his cattle if Hercules could do the job in one day, which he did. The cleansing of the Augean stables is Hercules' most intellectual labour, and one of the things that really endeared him to Romans.

The Romans were, after all, first conquerors and colonisers, but they were, secondly, really proficient engineers. They gave us running water, showers, flushes, clean dishes and fruit. The Romans, with their aqueducts and outdoor toilets, were really good at sending water in a useful direction.

Hercules diverted two rivers, Alpheus and Peneas, into the stables and the force of the river currents cleansed them, well within a twenty-four hour period. Augeas failed to give Hercules some cattle, as he had contracted. Outraged, Hercules killed Augeas and installed his son as king of that realm.

When Eurystheus met Hercules again outside the city walls, the king declared that the stable cleaning did not count as one of the official labours because the rivers had done all the work. Also, Hercules had accepted payment for what was supposed to be volunteer work, the king noted, even though the payment was never made.

The next labour was to remove the Stymphalian birds. They were named after the swamp in which they lived. These birds were a nightmare worthy of a Blumhouse production. Though they were only the size of cranes, they had bronze beaks, metal wings, and poison poop.

They fed on human crops, ravaging farmland. They were capable of dining on humans, as well. They did not even need to attack. Their metal feathers were like darts. These feathers, alone, could kill a man when dropped from any height. Going up against these animals with human strength and human weapons had proven futile. The birds simply pecked their enemies to death, and their beaks could pierce any kind of armour.

What worried Hercules the most about this assignment, however, was that the birds were sacred to the great war god, Mars. Juno had hated our hero from birth. Now he was making a new divine enemy.

The Stymphalian swamp would not hold Hercules' weight, so he could not, initially, get close to the birds. Minerva saw his dilemma and gave him a magic noise maker. You can think of this as a really loud baby rattle or perhaps a supernatural castanet. This he took to the peak of a nearby mountain, rattled it, setting off an ungodly racket with an echo to boot, and thus scared the birds into flight.

Once airborne, they were fair game for Hercules' poison arrows. Some of the birds escaped him, but they fled Arcadia. Hercules collected some of their corpses to show Eurystheus.

The Cretan Bull and the Mad Horses

The next mission was to capture and bring home the Cretan bull. This supernatural creature had already caused some trouble at Olympos' highest level. It was, originally, a gift to King Minos from Neptune, the ocean god.

In the bull's back story, Minos had prayed for an all-white bull to appear as a sign that he was the legitimate ruler of Crete, despite the existence of brothers who might have challenged his claim. Neptune was pleased with Minos' presumed piety, and he sent the white bull onto the scene. The bull was a perfect specimen, and Minos was supposed to sacrifice it to Neptune because the gods valued beauty and perfection in their sacrificial objects.

When Minos saw how beautiful the bull was, he declined to sacrifice it. If he had sought decent advice, perhaps from a seer or oracle or nymph or underworld resident, he would have predicted Neptune's outrage. Mortals have been destroyed for much smaller omissions.

Neptune infused the bull with his own righteous anger, and the beast proceeded to ravage Crete. But that was not enough damage. Neptune also caused Minos' wife, Pasiphaë, to fall madly in love with the bull. This was no platonic love; hiding herself inside a wooden cow, she managed to mate with the bull and soon became pregnant with the Minotaur who has his own story.

The Minotaur would eat nothing but human flesh (raw), so Minos charged the engineer Daedelus to construct a labyrinth that would hold the Minotaur and limit his damage. Young people were then sent into the labyrinth where they were devoured. Daedelus was, incidentally, the same engineer who had built the wooden cow for Pasiphaë.[4]

When Hercules showed up to capture the Cretan bull, Minos was all too ready to part with it. Hercules dispensed with the ritual of carrying the animal back to Tiryns himself. He sent it to Eurystheus in the care of messengers. The king did not manage to keep the bull captive. It broke away from Tiryns and ravaged the plains of Marathon.

Next up, Eurystheus sent Hercules to capture the human-flesh-eating female horses belonging to the Thracian king, Diomedes. Myth blends seamlessly into history when Alexander the Great is said to have had a horse named Bucephalus, descended from these mythic mares. The ancient poets have explained that the mares had gone mad from eating human flesh.

Diomedes was the son of the great war god, Mars. Nevertheless, he was an utter savage, replete with long, uncombed hair and tattoos that heralded his murderous accomplishments. The war-like inhabitants of Thrace were too wild to cooperate, one tribe with another, so they had no centralised government. Diomedes presided over the Bistones.

To prevent his sons from threatening his leadership, he had sold them into slavery in far-off lands.

The Bistones never turned any visitors away. Strangers and diplomatic envoys alike were offered hospitality and a chance to amuse Diomedes. When he tired of them, he fed them to his horses. Hercules knew of this treacherous custom, but he approached Diomedes with as much duplicity as he met with. Hercules played the part of the perfectly naive guest while Diomedes played the part of the perfect tribal host.

Diomedes offered his daughters for Hercules' sexual amusement. He assured Hercules that any children born of such union would not be sold, but honoured as a descendent of the famed Hercules. He declared this, even as he was planning to murder the baby daddy of his grandchildren.

'Thank you, but I would rather take a look at your famous mares', was more or less what Hercules said. Diomedes had no particular reason to refuse the request. After all, Hercules was going to end his visit as horse food, either way.

Abderus, the young man commissioned to lead Hercules to the stables, knew the hero and introduced himself. Abderus' ship had been attacked by pirates while he was traveling with his father. The young man was taken captive and subsequently traded as a slave to the Bistones. Because he knew how to handle horses, he had been recruited as a groom to the flesh-eating mares, a job he despised, especially as the horses had badly injured him. He showed Hercules the hand on which he had only two fingers left. Hercules promised to get him out of there.

In the meantime, Abderus provided some useful information: Diomedes had never attempted to ride the mad mares or even harness them to a chariot. They remained in their bronze mangers, tethered with metal chains. Only Diomedes could manage them, but even he had no control when they were hungry.

Upon entering the stable, Hercules saw bloodied walls and floor, along with the offal of Diomedes' visitors. The other animals were cowering in fear, afraid to sleep, even. When they saw Hercules, the man-eating mares reared and bit the air, but their chains held them.

Hercules found a young steer, clubbed it over the head and threw it to the mares. As they gathered over the corpse in a feeding frenzy, he clubbed the horses on the heads, not hard enough to kill them, but enough to knock them out. He unchained them, then led and harnessed them to a chariot which he and Abderus mounted. Using the strength of the recovered mares, the two men took off.

The wild team passed Diomedes' residence in its mad dash out of town, and the king pursued them. Hercules and Abderus crashed through the wooden village gates and headed to Tyrins. Diomedes had gathered a posse to catch them, however, so Hercules hid the horses, noting that they were exhausted, and left them in the care of Abderus while he backtracked to deal with Diomedes. It was not his intention to kill the man. After all, Diomedes was the son of Mars, however perverse he had become. So he tapped the savage king with his club, knocked him out, and carried him back to the mares.

Hercules was horrified to find Abderus dead and partially consumed. He had lost control of the horses. Enraged, Hercules threw Diomedes at the flock of mares. They did not stop to consider that he was their master. They tore at him with their teeth and trampled him under their hooves. Then they were still.

Was it consuming Diomedes' rage that tamed the horses? All we know is that by the time they reached Eurystheus, the horses were no longer mad carnivores. Eventually, they would be freed to wander as high as Mount Olympos, where they were killed by other divine beasts.

Hercules and Theseus

At this point in time, Hercules' story collides with that of another Roman hero, Theseus. Theseus was conceived during a brief affair and raised by his mother only. His father was either Neptune or Aegeus, the king of Athens. He volunteered as tribute when it came time to sacrifice young Athenian men and women to the Minotaur. King Minos had established the tribute to punish his enemies and mollify his weird stepson, this half-man, half-beast that roamed the labyrinth Daedelus had designed.

Annually, the young men and women were dumped in the labyrinth; either they were eaten by the Minotaur or they got lost in the maze and died of dehydration. However, that would not be Theseus' fate. Theseus was another darling of the gods and under the protection of Venus, amongst others. To ensure that her hero could survive the labyrinth,

Venus made Ariadne fall madly in love with him, 'madly' being the operative word in this context.

Ariadne begged the engineer, Daedelus, to give her something that would help Theseus, and he gave her a ball of magic string. It turned out to be as easy as that to kill the Minotaur. Once in the labyrinth, Theseus unspooled the thread, as he meandered down the twisting passages of the dungeon. The thread ran out, right at the entrance to the centre chamber where the monster was sleeping.

Theseus jumped the creature with all his might and the Minotaur awoke. The two were matched in strength, and wrestled for some time. But eventually, the Minotaur tired and Theseus was able to kill him. He found his way back to Ariadne and the other tributes using the magic string.

Ariadne got the Athenian teenagers onto a ship and the tributes snuck out of Crete under the cloak of night. Iolaus, Hercules' nephew, was on that ship. Hercules had left him in Crete, trusting that he would get home on his own, which he did, eventually.

The escapees made a safe landing in Naxos, where Theseus went on to his next adventure without Ariadne. Theseus' abandonment of her is so famous that Richard Strauss wrote an opera about it. According to at least one source, Bacchus appeared to Theseus in a dream and told him to back off because he was in love with Ariadne himself. But your humble author knows that Theseus never fell in love with Ariadne. He saw himself as the world's hero, but he had been saved by a girl. He couldn't live with the dissonance.

Iolaus found his way back to Hercules and told the story of young Theseus' triumphs. It was timely information because Hercules had been assigned his next labour and he was assembling a team.

Admete, Eurystheus' daughter, was the architect of the next labour. She was not a bloody-minded girl, but she may have had a crush on Hercules. He inspired a lot of that. She asked her father for the golden belt belonging to Hippolyta, queen of the Amazons. As she had hoped, Eurystheus turned her request into one of the labours.

Sometimes referred to as a girdle, this belt was worn on the outside of Hippolyta's clothes as decor and a symbol of power. It was the kind of belt more often worn by powerful men. Mercury had bestowed it on her, so of course it was magic.

Artists tend to depict it as a wide belt with an elaborate engraved metal buckle. An oil painting by Nicolaus Knüpfer shows Hippolyta wrestling rather half-heartedly with Hercules over the belt while she is dressed in the finery of the Dutch golden age: silk dress, fur wrap, and pearl earrings. It really doesn't look like a fight to the death, raising the question: When Hippolyta saw Theseus, did she throw the game? He would eventually be her husband, after all.

Hercules understood that he could not go up against the Amazons alone. He wished to recruit Theseus, and so he travelled to Athens to see if he could convince the hero who had defeated the Minotaur to take on yet another heroic endeavour. Upon entering Athens, he learned that Theseus was now king of that city, his father having recently died.

Hercules' fame had, by now, travelled all over the civilised world, and Theseus volunteered for the mission immediately, despite his duties as king. He also provided Hercules with ships. The wrestling champion, Peleus, and his brother, Telemon, joined the adventure, making it officially a quest.

Word spread quickly through the city-state that the great son of Jupiter was assembling a band of champions. So many men applied that Hercules had to turn it into a competition. He tested the applicants' running, climbing, and rowing skills, choosing only the strongest and sturdiest. Among the successful applicants were Autolycus, Deilion and Plogios.

Everyone in Hercules' crew had double or triple duty. Except for Theseus, they all rowed and, when encountering an enemy, they must also fight. Theseus sat in the steerman's seat, and he sometimes regaled the rowers by playing his lyre. Hercules rowed.

The party made land at the city of Paros where Minos' grandson, Alcaios, ruled as king, alongside his noble brother, Sthenelos. Theseus declined to get off the ship and hunt with Hercules. He feared that Minos' fury might have tracked him even to this remote spot.

This fear proved well founded a few minutes later. Two men of Hercules' crew went to find water, and they encountered four men of Paros. They were sons of Minos. The questers naively explained that they were traveling with Theseus and Hercules on a mission of urgency, and they were murdered for their troubles. Their bodies were found broken in a ravine.

Minos' sons next tracked down Hercules' camp and were preparing to murder the rest of the crew when Hercules returned from his hunt. He saw the broken bodies of his crew and flew into a rage, killing three of the murderers almost instantly with his club. The other one he shot with an arrow.

King Alcaios next showed up at camp with a formal welcome party, but he was startled to find it the site of a small massacre. When he had assessed the situation, he was quick to distance himself from Minos and compliment Theseus on his victory over the Minotaur. Hercules' rage at the murder of his companions was still fresh, and the situation quickly turned into a diplomatic problem.

Hercules noted that etiquette had been badly breached and that he could, in all justice, tear the town apart. The young, fat Alcaios was in way over his head, but he acted quickly to avert disaster. He forgave the death of his uncles immediately; in his private opinion, they were outlaws, as he explained out loud. His own loyalty to Minos was minimal, he averred. Finally, he offered Hercules any two men of his kingdom to replace the two murdered crew members.

With no hesitation, Hercules said he would take the brothers Alcaios and Sthenelos. Sthenelos was tremendously pleased at being promoted to Hercules' companion as any man of spirit would be. Alcaios protested that he had a kingdom to rule, but Hercules renewed his threat to take the city by violence.

Minos' grandson meditated briefly on his lack of an army, weapons, and fortifications of any kind. Paros was protected by little more than Minos' reputation, Alcaios suddenly realised. So he made the best of it and agreed to join the quest. Hercules' terrifying anger was finally mollified, and he promised to return the grandsons of Minos to Paros safely, when the quest was accomplished.

Hercules and Theseus did obtain the belt from Hippolyta, but how? Poets have declined to agree. Some say Juno disguised herself as an Amazon and stirred up hostilities against the heroes. Some say Hippolyta was killed during the ensuing conflict. But we have had so much bloodshed, haven't we?

So let us cast our minds on Shakespeare's *Midsummer Night's Dream*, ever so loosely based on Ovid, in which Theseus returns to

Athens with his fiancée, Hippolyta. She has gracefully surrendered her belt and agreed to combine her power with that of Athen's king. She has no difficulty with language barriers, and she fits right into Elizabethan women's clothing with no discomfort and no urge to display her tattoos or piercings. She is in love; her life with her Amazonian sisters is a distant dream. (I did say this was loosely based on Ovid, didn't I?)

'I wooed thee with my sword', Theseus says to Hippolyta in a tender Shakespearean moment. 'But I will wed thee in another key/With pomp, with triumph, and with reveling.'[5]

The name 'Hippolyta', in Greek could be translated 'Unleash the horses!' Shakespeare's Hippolyta brings a timely liberation to the people of Athens who are oblivious to the conflicts Theseus and Hercules have been through. She sagely advises Theseus on how to deal with Athenians, whose petty quarrels he must now adjudicate. Fresh from war, Theseus is so enamoured of his Amazon queen that he grants her every wish, and peace reigns in Athens. Hercules is nowhere to be seen. He has moved on to another grinding labour.

Geryon

Since we like to cast him as the villain, Eurystheus may have been disgusted at how easily Hercules obtained the belt from Hippolyta. Two pretty boys and a bunch of single women. Both of them were musicians, skilled in the lyre. What had he been thinking?

Casting his mind over all the really ugly monsters out there, he landed on the idea of sending Hercules up against Geryon. This unfortunate giant was effectively conjoined triplets. Geryon had two legs which supported three heads and torsos. Artists often represent him with one very cut torso and three heads, however, perhaps because it's just slightly more viable, anatomically speaking.

Wikipedia describes him as 'mostly humanoid'; he was as human as you might expect him to be considering his mother was Medusa (she of snake-hair fame). His only companions were his two-headed dog, a litter mate of the hellhound Cerberus, and his shepherd, Eurytion. By most accounts, Geryon minded his own business and represented a threat to no one. However he owned some very fine red cattle which Eurystheus coveted. So he sent Hercules to steal these excellent specimens.

Geryon lived in the remote land of Erytheia, which even the most determined of classicist cartographers have been unable to pinpoint. Most agree that it is some part of modern-day Spain.[6] Hercules needed the help of the gods in locating Geryon, and he got it, eventually.

Crossing an African desert, he suffered heat exhaustion and shot an arrow at the sun in symbolic frustration. The sun god could have been offended. He could have sent a solar flare to kill Hercules instantly. But he did not. Most of the gods loved Hercules and despised Juno. So, instead of striking him dead for heresy, the sun god gave Hercules a magic cup.

This cup helped the sun god cross the seas swiftly and with no effort. Hercules used it to find Geryon's island, which was otherwise impossible for a mere mortal to find because Geryon lived beyond the known world. According to a minor Greek poet, Pherecydes, Hercules was searching for Geryon across the seas when the old god, Oceanus, made trouble by churning up the waves. Hercules responded by telling the titan to stop or he would feel the sting of Hercules' arrows.

The old god retreated under the waves and stopped his mischief. This minor Hercules' story may have had particular appeal to the Romans because it suggests that Hercules is a company man. He supports the new generation of gods against the old ones who are more chaotic and unpredictable. Because the Romans valued order in government and obedience among their citizens, they saw in Hercules a hero who embodied their values.

When Hercules made land, Geryon was ready for him. He made a formidable sight with helmets on all three heads and shields and spears in all six hands. His shepherd and dog ran ahead of him to fight Hercules on the shore. With his club, Hercules killed both of them. When he finally spotted Geryon running at him and roaring with three mouths, Hercules could not help laughing. It was an inopportune time for finding humour however, because it gave Geryon seconds in which to pick up huge boulders and throw them. Hercules dodged the rocks which mostly landed in the sea.

Arrows dipped in hydra blood were very handy for shooting Geryon in all three heads, quickly. The giant fell near the beach, and Hercules

Hercules was sent to serve the Libyan Queen Omphale as a punishment for stealing the sacred tripod. Artists often portray it as an erotic adventure, and Rubens' work is no exception. (Public Domain)

This painting visualises Jupiter's descent into Danae's chamber as a cloud of gold. Her nurse, who seems not to understand what this scene is about, is attempting to capture the gold in a bag. (Public Domain)

This vase painting shows Hercules breaking an antler off the sacred hind in the presence of Minerva and Diana. It's a good illustration of Hercules' relationship to the gods. They applaud his temerity and strength, but here they show up to ensure that he does not go too far. (Public Domain)

Right: Cacus was a specifically Roman god who spewed smoke and fire like a dragon. Here Hercules is pictured killing him with his club. (Public Domain)

Below: Hercules famously chose virtue and duty over fun. Here, Virtue looks a lot like Minerva in armour. She is pointing the way he must go if he wishes a noble life. (Public Domain)

Few artists really wanted to show a brave Roman hero murdering a woman for her accessory, but de Rossi went there. Here, Hercules is about to club Hippolyta to death for her belt. (Public Domain)

Right: The Garden of the Hesperides was a myth within a myth. Here three goddesses guard the golden apples that Hercules was required to steal. (Public Domain)

Below: Fabre gave his audience the complete Judgment of Paris. Venus is pictured with her illegitimate son, Cupid. It appears that Paris has accepted her bribe and declared her the most fair, to the outrage of Juno – with her peacock and Minerva – in armour. Someone has dropped a torch. (Public Domain)

Famed actress Sarah Bernhardt played Medea on stage. This theatre poster captures her with a bloody knife and an arm tattoo. (Public Domain)

Above: In the Aeneid, Dido falls on her sword after Aeneas leaves Carthage. On her right, a servant discovers her dead body. On her left, the rainbow goddess, Iris, takes her soul to the underworld. (Public Domain)

Right: This narratively useful painting shows Jupiter seducing Leda while he is in the form of a swan. On the ground are the four children she bore after this union: Castor, Pollux, Helen, and Clytemnestra. They seem to have hatched out of swan eggs. I leave that to the reader's imagination. (Public Domain)

Perseus is vividly captured here, using the head of Medusa to turn his opponents to stone. Notice how he keeps his eyes on the floor. (Photo courtesy of Pixabay)

Laocoon was right about Greeks bearing gifts, but the gods wanted Troy to fall, so they sent snakes to kill Laocoon and his two sons. (Public Domain)

Left: This painting captures the way ancient Romans saw Mercury. He sees a pretty girl and swoops down from the sky. (Public Domain)

Below: In this painting, Picot captures Cupid's secret marriage to Psyche. He is leaving her in the morning before she can wake up and identify him. (Public Domain)

Above: This painting uses simultaneous narrative, meaning it shows us several different moments in the story at the same time. It shows us the moment that Actaeon happens on Diana, naked with her following, the moment she is about to splash water on him, the moment he sprouts antlers, and the moment one of his dogs catches a whiff of him. (Public Domain)

Right: Bernini famously sculpted Daphne as she was turning into a tree to escape Apollo's passion. (Public Domain)

Aeneas is pictured here with his elderly and disabled father, Anchises. Anchises was too debilitated to leave Troy, so Aeneas carried him. (Public Domain)

Without the help of the river god Tiber, Aeneas might never have completed his quest to settle in western Italy. Tiber, left, with river weeds in his hair, tells Aeneas to seek help from Evander. (Public Domain)

Above: Perseus is pictured here
saving Andromeda from the sea
monster who is variously presented
as a dragon, snake, giant squid,
kraken, or toothful eel. Many artists
portrayed Perseus on a winged
horse, but this one went back to
the classical sources and shows
our hero with winged sandals and
helmet. (Public Domain)

Right: The Renaissance artists didn't
entirely approve of decadence.
Caravaggio gives us a young, highly
feminised Bacchus. As you expect,
he has leaves in his hair and a glass
of wine. But take a good look at
the fruit, and you will see that it is
largely rotted. (Public Domain)

This updated image of Medusa captures her essential innocence. (Public Domain)

Sandys portrayed Medea much as Flaccus saw her: highly anxious and conflicted about helping Jason. She is pictured here concoting a potion of some kind. Note the frog on the table. (Public Domain)

Right: This lively drawing finds the celebrity musician Orpheus leading his wife Eurydice out of the underworld. She has narrowly escaped the three-headed Cerberus, visible in the lower left corner. (Public Domain)

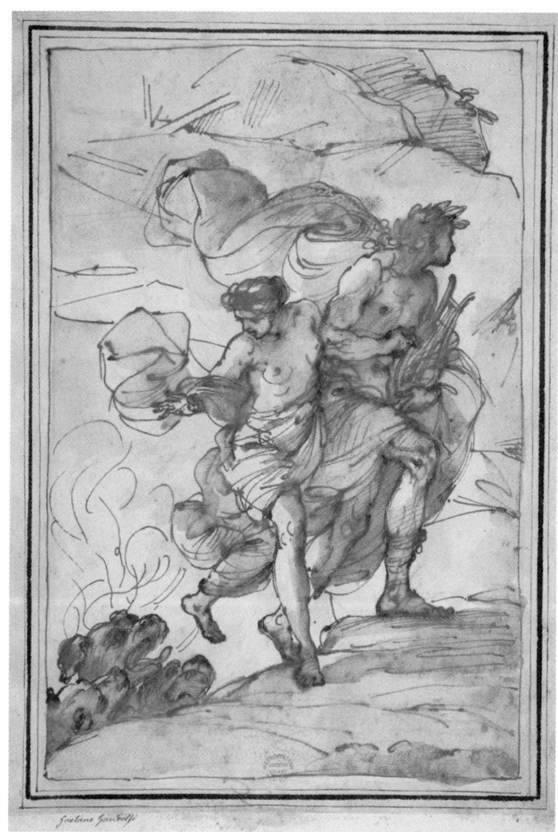

Below: Ulysses swam home from his most recent shipwreck. Minerva disguised him, so that he would not be murdered by his wife's suitors. But she didn't change his smell. So his old dog recognised him. (Public Domain)

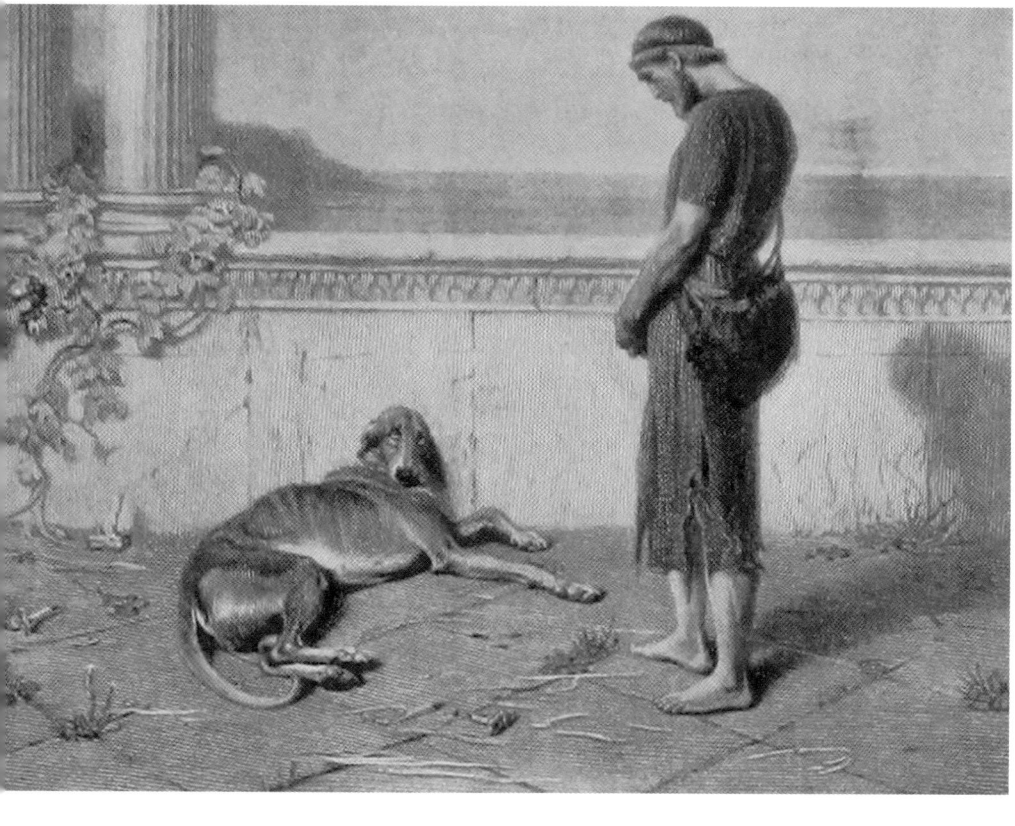

As the Greeks were burning Troy to the ground, Ajax dragged the priestess Cassandra out of Minerva's temple. Minerva didn't take this desecration as a harmless prank. You can see her icon in the background of the painting, looking pretty grim. She would personally kill Ajax with a lightning bolt. (Public Domain)

started the long trip back to Tiryns with a huge herd of cattle. The journey took them past the Italian hill of Aventine. There, the monster, Cacus, captured four steers and four cows out of the herd and hid the animals in his cave while Hercules was sleeping.

Cacus was a powerful immortal, the son of Vulcan, that Olympian metal smith who chose to live in his forge. Vulcan gave Cacus the genetic gift of breathing fire and smoke. He was also a terrorist cannibal who nailed the heads of the humans he killed on the outside of his cave.

Hercules might not have missed those eight heads of cattle. He was a big picture kind of guy. But the long, long trip back to Tiryns took him right past Cacus' cave. One of the captive cows cried out, and the herd answered her, pausing in their distress. Cacus had enough sense to be scared, and he blocked off the entrance to his cave with a boulder.

Furious, Hercules tore off the top of the mountain and exposed the monster to the sky. Cacus tried to exhale enough smoke to hide himself, but it availed him little. Hercules threw trees and giant rocks at him. Finally, our hero threw himself into the thickest part of the smoke and found Cacus. According to Virgil, Hercules grasped Cacus so hard by the throat that his eyes popped out of his head and the blood left his neck. No more would the cannibal roam the hills of Italy, preying on the unwary.

The Golden Apples and the Underworld

You might say that Eurystheus had given up on monsters. None of them so far had defeated Hercules. The last of Hercules' labours sent him to places that no mortal is intended to find. There are myths within myths, and the Hesperides are much like Schrodinger's cat: both real and imaginary at the same time.

Like the Graces and Muses, the Hesperides are a small group of immortal females who are personified and purely symbolic at the same time. Artists like to portray them all the same height and very similar in appearance, almost always in Grecian drapes or long flowing dresses.

Some say they are the daughters of Atlas, he who willingly holds the heavens on his back. Some say they are the daughters of Night. They are women, yes, but together they are also the sunset. One of the goddesses provides the pink/orange hues, one the blue of sky, and another provides the gold of the sun.

The Hesperides live in the far, far west, and there they guard the golden apples which the titan Terra gave to Juno on her wedding day. No man knows where that land is, no man can find the home of the Hesperides any more than a man can hold a sunset in his hand. And that is where Eurystheus commanded Hercules to go.

'Bring me three of the golden apples of the Hesperides', he ordered.

Hercules reasoned that demigods ought to know one another, so he located some nymphs playing on a river bank. He asked them how to find the Hesperides, and they referred him on to Nereus, a powerful sea god who could take many shapes. 'You can't miss him', nymphs sang out, approximately. 'He is quite elderly, has a weirdly long grey beard and blue hair. Also, he has fifty daughters who like to dance with him.'

Hercules sought out this deity on the banks of the Aegean Sea. But Nereus saw him coming and changed himself into a black lobster. Undeceived, Hercules lifted him up and threatened to dash him to pieces on some nearby rocks. Nereus then took the form of a huge brown bull, but Hercules grabbed him by the horns so firmly that there was no escaping him. Finally, Nereus told Hercules what he must do.

Those instructions took our hero to the top of a tall mountain in Africa where he found the titan Atlas, father of the Hesperides. This is the same Atlas that Perseus petrified. Lamentably, dear reader, I do the best I can, but there are different versions. In this story, Atlas was still conscious and speaking. He was also holding up the sky, as he was fated to do. Hercules asked Atlas to tell him where the Hesperides were. Atlas, stooped and tired, gave this a minute's thought and then said something very like, 'Hold the sky for me; I will go get them myself'.

You smell a trap. I smell a trap. Hercules almost certainly smelled a trap. But what could he do? He never did find the land of sunset. Atlas, finally freed of his burden, darted over there and got the apples himself. The mistake he made was returning to Hercules. 'Who wants these apples?' Atlas asked.

'Eurystheus, King of Tiryns.'

'Where would I find him?'

'Hey, I don't mind holding up the sky, but I have a terrible backache. Could you just hold it for me while I pad out my cloak?' was close to what Hercules said. For a big man, he was clever.

Atlas, not as much. He took the sky back, and that was the last time he got a break from it. Hercules picked up the apples and walked off, maybe whistling, maybe not.

Back in Tiryns, Eurystheus had carefully considered where to send Hercules if he came back. The gods had not permitted him to fail, so far, but there was a place that humans never came back from, and that was the land of the dead.

The descent into the underworld was a rite of passage for Roman heroes. You have already seen Orpheus do it and return, but only at great cost. Ulysses and Aeneas would also descend and be among the rare mortals to return to the world of the living.

Hercules' final labour would be to plunder this underworld and bring the hellhound Cerberus to the land of the living. This was the perfect labour. It involved going where no man could go, capturing a monster that no one could handle, and risking the eternal wrath of the gods. Pluto would not tolerate the violation of his rules and his kingdom, Eurystheus reasoned. Even if he could steal Cerberus, Hercules would be charged with heresy.

But the gods had chosen sides, and most of them sided with Hercules. Even Juno was under orders not to kill him, and these orders came from Jupiter, her husband, king, and brother. Hercules took off for Arcadia where he found a cold poisonous stream that flowed into a river, then plunged straight down into the earth.

This was the River Styx, one of Hades' rivers. Some poets say that nothing can survive the Styx, that it dissolves iron and anything else that has the misfortune to be thrown at it. Into this torrent, Hercules threw himself. It took him to the Stygian Lake where he saw the ferryman of the dead, an immortal named Charon.

No one can pass the gates of Hades without being ferried by Charon. It was customary for an individual to bring him some kind of payment. To that end, people who believed in Charon would bury their folk with a coin, exact change to pay this old pilot.

He was not a thing of beauty. His clothes were ragged and dirty, his beard long and unkempt, his visage hideous. People need to fear death; otherwise, they get careless.

'You're alive', Charon said to Hercules.

'Well spotted. I need to steal Cerberus', Hercules said, more or less. 'It's the will of the gods. It's the will of Jupiter, in particular.'

'I'm not helping', might have been the reply.

Hercules dispensed with words and just jumped into the boat. Terrified, Charon mounted no further arguments. To the gates of hell they rowed. Cerberus was waiting there with his three heads. His jaws were the stuff of nightmares.

But, according to the nineteenth-century mythologist Charles Kingsley, the dog was more bark than bite. Cerberus was used to harmless, hopeless 'shades' of no substance. Yet here was Hercules, all hard muscle and real sweat. Cerberus backed away from him all the way to the throne of Pluto, where the dog lay down at his king's feet.[7] 'Are you crazy?' was something Pluto might have asked. According to Kingsley, he recognised Hercules immediately.

Hercules looked up at the great god of the afterlife on his throne. 'No', Hercules would have replied. 'I am here to steal Cerberus and take him to where the sun does shine.'

In the end, Pluto did not give Hercules much of an argument. The gods had permitted him all the other atrocities he had committed. Why balk at this one?

His visit to the underworld threw Hercules together with Theseus again. Theseus had been trapped in the land of the dead for several years, having travelled there to help his friend, Pirithous. The two had hatched a mad plan to kidnap Proserpina, with whom Pirithous fancied himself in love.

They hadn't just failed, they had gotten themselves trapped in the underworld with no hope of returning.[8] Pluto had invited them to partake of refreshment, then seated them in the Chair of Forgetfulness. Once seated, Theseus and his friend found that snakes came out of nowhere and wrapped themselves around the men's legs, preventing them from leaving. Hercules was able to liberate Theseus, but Pirithous' bonds were too strong, perhaps because emotionally, he was unable to surrender his dream of Proserpina.

Theseus returned to his wife, Phaedra, and their son, Hippolytus. By this time, he had murdered Hippolyta in order to make a better political marriage. Hercules presented Eurystheus with the dog, then took the beast back down to Pluto's throne where he belonged. The labours, finally, were over.

The Madness; the Murders

Please bear in mind that an exact timeline for Hercules is impossible to construct because of major and minor changes to the story enacted by every new poet that took on yet another remake. Most notably, perhaps, some writers have Hercules going mad and killing his first family early on in his career. In that version of the Hercules' story, the labours are god-ordained penance for his crime. However, Seneca's Hercules performs all twelve labours before Juno makes him insane.

While Hercules was in the underworld, a banished criminal named Lycus captured Megara, Hercules' wife, and her father, King Creon of Thebes. Creon had exiled Lycus for antisocial behaviour; now Lycus took advantage of Hercules' absence to claim his vengeance.

Lycus knew that he could not hold Creon's kingdom for long without a royal connection. The solution to this problem? He must marry Megara, Hercules' wife, and claim her greatness by association for himself. No one would defy Megara's husband, Lycus calculated. She was a king's daughter and a hero's consort. For her own part, Megara retreated to a holy altar inside a temple where she prayed for protection against Lycus.

When she saw Lycus approaching, Megara quickly said she would rather die than marry him. He replied that Hercules was nothing better than a slave, doing whatever madness Eurystheus commanded. And killing monsters doesn't make a hero, he added. Megara countered that there is courage in overcoming what most men fear.

Next, Lycus tried outright heresy, claiming that neither Juno nor Eurystheus had ordered the labours. Hercules did all that destruction on his own initiative. Then he threatened to rape Megara. When she repelled him again, he ordered his servants to burn down the temple in which she had sought sanctuary. One pyre should be enough to kill

Megara and all her children, he guessed. Amphitryon asked to die first and be spared the sight of Megara dying as well as his grandchildren.

That was the scene Hercules walked into when he returned from the underworld. He had hoped to come home to a loving family tableau, but now his father and children were dressed in rags and his wife in mourning garments. Clearly, his family had suffered a catastrophe.

Meanwhile, Juno was plotting more mischief. She knew that her obsession with Hercules had made him both successful and famous. If she had not pitched so many lethal challenges his way, he would be an unknown bastard. Instead, he is now the hero of impossible challenges. The gods needed Hercules to become the hero whose grandeur would polish the lustre on their icons, Juno mused.

At the same time, she debated within herself, Hercules had grown so powerful that he represented a danger to the gods. Surely he would challenge heaven! Bacchus, another of Jupiter's illegitimate sons with a mortal woman, had become a powerful god. Juno acknowledged as much. Bacchus came to Olympos in peace, but Hercules 'will seek a path through ruin, and will desire to rule in an empty universe', she declared.

Was Juno really worried about the Olympians' regime, or was she just still angry about Jupiter's affair with Alcmene? The poets generally agreed that Juno was not allowed to kill Hercules directly, but Seneca captures, in particular, how much she chafed as that instruction: 'crush this plotter of big things . . . thyself rend him in pieces with thine own hands. Why to another entrust such hate?' she laments, seeming to have very few constraints against her.[9]

In Hercules' story, Juno had always been the wizard behind the curtain. She is the unambiguous villain with an anger so petty and vindictive, even the most pious of ancient poets had trouble defending her. As the Roman gods often did, she favoured individuals who were well placed to make her enemy's life a living hell. But her pet, Eurystheus, was despised by the poets, their readers, and anyone else who admired Hercules and wished him well. That was pretty much everyone except Juno. Eurystheus' was tarnished with the same brush that made Juno a powerful, but hated force of nature.

It was time for Juno to enact her greatest crime, so far, against Hercules. Not content with just any torment, she summoned a goddess buried deep in the recesses of the underworld. The goddess' name was Discord and she threw a lock of her snaky hair into Hercules' chest, where it nestled like a serpent and instantly made him insane.

Right after he had killed the usurper, Lycus, Hercules felt the onset of madness. His children looked like Lycus' children, so he killed several of them. Megara he confused with Juno. In *Hercules Furens*, the reader can hear her beg for her life. She had one son with her, and she asked Hercules to notice how much the boy looked like his father. Still under the spell of madness, Hercules gave his son such a violent look, the boy died before Hercules even touched him. Megara he clubbed to death, crushing her bones and decapitating her in his fury.

Amphitryon, seeing the carnage, instructed Hercules to kill him next. He played into his stepson's madness saying, 'See, a victim stands before the altar . . . he awaits the stroke. I offer myself to death'.[10] But Hercules was finally exhausted from his rampage. He fell asleep, his madness short lived and now waning. He awoke with his senses fully restored, but he had no memory of recent events.

Soon, though, he recognised the bodies of his murdered children and demanded to know who killed them. Theseus and Amphitryon at first hesitated to tell him. They must, though. Amphitryon gently led his stepson through the first stage of grief, assuring him that this massacre was the work of Juno, and that Hercules should not bear the guilt. Theseus offered Hercules a home in Athens, the city he ruled.[11]

Omphale

It is not entirely certain when Hercules travelled to Lydia and had his adventure with Omphale, but your humble author likes to believe it happened after his madness, as a matter of justice.

A beautiful painting by Flemish painter Peter Paul Rubens shows Omphale tugging playfully on Hercules' ear while he holds her distaff, a weaving implement. Musicians perform in the near background, while an old woman, further back, flips a gesture that was widely taken to mean 'cuckold' in the early 1600s.

In Rubens' masterpiece, Hercules is completely naked, his lion skin and club have been discarded nearby (but they are still in the picture because that was artist code for 'This be Hercules'). It is obvious that Rubens intended to show Omphale's dominance over the legendary hero.

The lightweight domestic fray in which he finds himself makes his extreme musculature distinctly out of sync. But human musculature was Rubens' great talent, so the muscles are painstakingly spelled out with shadows and contouring. How did the great Hercules find himself in this diminished and preposterous condition? Last time we saw him, Theseus had offered him a home in Athens.

Sometime after the death of his wife and children, Hercules discovered that his old enemy, King Eurystheus, had staged an archery contest; he had also advertised that he would give his beautiful daughter, Iole, to the winner. Hearts must have sunk when Hercules showed up on the playing field. Who could defeat him? His height and musculoskeletal system would have discouraged the strongest and most accomplished athletes gathered.

Hercules played by the rules and defeated Eurystheus and all his sons as well as any other contestants. At the end of the competition, he claimed his prize: marriage to the beautiful Iole. Eurystheus refused to honour his contract, however; out loud, he noted that Hercules had killed his last wife. Finally, Hercules had a good enough reason to kill this tyrant. So he did. Iole became, not his wife, but his sex slave, to pay for Eurystheus' many crimes.

As he had done before, more than once, Hercules sought out a priestess to absolve him of a killing. This time, he sought absolution for killing his kinsman, Eurystheus. But the particular Delphic priestess that he consulted was either too scared of Hercules or too disgusted to give him any advice. Hercules is not a man known for biding his time or controlling his temper. Outraged that the priestess was not doing her job, he began destroying the temple.

Then he saw the Delphic tripod, a mostly useless piece of furniture that was, nevertheless, extremely sacred to the gods. Within moments, the gods had chosen sides and were, literally, fighting each other over the tripod. Would Hercules get away with stealing it? Let the bickering begin. Apollo, the god of Delphi, and his sister Diana attempted to pull it away from Hercules. (Remember that Apollo and Diana were half siblings to Hercules, and this detail becomes substantially more Norman Rockwell.)

Minerva sided with our hero, however, and was helping him steal it. The sides were too well-matched, and it appeared they might be caught in a never-ending struggle, so Jupiter came down to earth from Olympos and parted them by hurling lightning between them. After that highly unbecoming family feud, it was decided that Hercules would go to distant Lydia, approximately where Turkey is today, and serve as Queen Omphale's servant. It was supposed to be a punishment, but then it was not. The servant became the lover, and his 'service' was nominal.

Lydians spoke their own Anatolian language. That Lydian tongue is extinct now, but a few inscriptions on coins and unearthed graffiti prove that it once moved and breathed. Their failure to read and write in either Greek or Latin made the Lydians barbarians, as far as the Greeks were concerned, and fair targets for lecherous humour as far as the Romans cared. One thing all the ancients agreed: Omphale was queen of this crude kingdom, and she was a great, great beauty. This lesser documented passage in our hero's life opens a pathway for more recent poets and artists to put Hercules in some erotic, even faintly compromising positions.

In 1724, Francois Lemoyne painted our hero, again consorting with his 'master', Omphale. He is holding her spinning gear as in Rubens' work, but he is looking into her face with longing. She is looking back at him, her dress falling past her hips, either deliberately, or it wasn't put on very securely to begin with.

Her alabaster body is perfect, at least by eighteenth-century standards. Cupid, sitting just to the right of this scene, is looking straight into the eyes of the viewer, breaking that fourth wall, while the lovers are lost in each other's gazes. Despite his seeming childlike innocence, Cupid has done some damage here, and he wants us to know that he knows.

Were they married? On this point, you can make up your own mind, because of the, ahem, multiple versions. But it is hard to take his enslavement seriously.

Death

Seneca's *Hercules Oetaeus* finds Hercules in central Greece, having married Deianira, a Greek princess. Beautiful Iole and her maidens were still his captives.

'I have crushed all who merited thy bolts. But to me, father, is heaven still denied?' he queried of his father, Jupiter. He was not praying for death, per se. Humans had been granted immortality, and Hercules knew it. Psyche and Tithonus became immortal because they were loved by the gods. Ganymede, a favourite lover of Jupiter, was taken to Olympos and deified directly as a child or even baby, depending on your artist.

Having defeated most of the monsters that were terrorising the civilized world, Hercules was now ready for his reward: eternal life in the company of the Olympians. He does not expect it to be easy. To clarify that point, he tells Jupiter, 'I ask thee not to show the way to me; but grant thy permission, father, and the way I'll find'.[12]

Deianira, meanwhile, was mad with jealousy over Iole even though Hercules had not moved to make her his wife. Iole herself assumed that she would become Deianira's servant. Unsure of her status in Hercules' life, Deianira committed the ultimate marital treason by praying to Juno and asking to be the instrument to destroy Hercules.

Her nurse, a companion with powerful witchcraft, tried to reason with her, but Deianira pushed back. She was outraged that Iole might have children with Hercules; the thought of them playing with her own children confounded her. She manifested the fury of a woman scorned. Hercules, she declared, would now have a worse problem than the hydra: a jealous wife.

Deianira's memory drifted back to the time when the centaur, Nessus, tried to steal her from Hercules. Husband and wife had been fording a flooded river, and Nessus agreed to take Deianira across on his back for a fee. Hercules, for his part, was stomping through the flood, and he fell behind. Nessus mistakenly thought he could kidnap Hercules' wife and make her his.

One arrow from our hero's bow dispatched the centaur. As the blood flowed from his body, Nessus caught some of it, using his hoof as a container. This collection of blood he gave to Deianira, promising her that it would work as a love charm, should she ever have a rival for Hercules' affection: 'A garment, smeared with this very gore, shalt thou give to him, if ever a hated mistress should usurp thy chamber', Nessus said as he was dying.[13]

Nessus told her not to expose the blood to sunlight. She had, therefore, been keeping it in a dark chamber of the palace. Now, she told her nurse where it was and asked her to retrieve it. With the centaur's blood, Deianira anointed a robe hastily stitched together by her maidens, and her nurse added some evil enchantments for good measure.

Deianira prayed to Cupid to restore Hercules' love to her, and she asked him specifically to use big strong arrows, because lightweight arrows would not budge him. Then she entrusted the robe to her servant, Lichas, who presented it to Hercules as a gift, made by her own hands.

Did Deianira subconsciously intend to kill Hercules? Seneca certainly hints that she was making bad choices out of jealousy. Could she really not have known that Nessus had been shot with an arrow poisoned by the hydra? Did she not suspect that the poison had infected his blood?

Deianira 'tested' the poisoned robe. When she threw it down on the ground in full sun, it quivered and convulsed, flaming up. So she had many reasons not to trust Nessus, not the least of which was that he attempted to kidnap and rape her.

Hercules ascended a steep, cloud-swept cliff to a remote temple of Jupiter. There he put on the robe and began praying. A groan escaped him. This would not be a sudden death. It seems to have taken hours. That single groan gave way to screams of pain and terror. His servants fled, but Hercules found Lichas, the servant who had unwittingly brought the robe. The boy grabbed onto the altar, in vain hope that he would be spared. He died of fear, however, before Hercules even touched him.

Of course, Hercules tried to remove the robe, but it had soldered itself onto his skin. Great chunks of his flesh came out as he tore at it. In his death throes, he could see, now, that it was Deianira behind the poison garment. He was outraged that, after killing so many seemingly immortal monsters, he was now dying at the hands of a woman.

If a woman were to take him down, it should have been Juno, he complained. This kind of death threw all his achievements into doubt: 'Now will Amphitryon be deemed my sire'.[14] He prayed to Jupiter to kill him with a thunderbolt. When that prayer failed, he asked for death by a lesser god: Minerva, Bellona, Mars, one of the Titans. For the first time in his life, he wept.

Alcmena, Hercules' mother, found him, but his situation was hopeless. The robe was gone, 'consumed with me', he explained. He asked someone to bring him his bow and arrows, preparing to kill himself. Then he passed out, and Alcmena instructed the servants to take his weapons away.

His son, Hyllus, appeared to say that Deianira had killed herself. Hercules came out of his swoon imagining that he had been taken to heaven. 'Juno calls me son!' he cried, but this delightful fantasy quickly abandoned him.[15] To Hyllus, he confided that he had taken Iole as a lover. Hyllus was to marry the poor girl, who had been robbed of her homeland, and raise any child she bore as his own, Hercules commanded his son.

Hercules' death was so prolonged that a pyre was built, and he threw himself on it, still alive. His screams stopped, and he found the section of fire that was burning brightest and hottest. Then he stood in that section. Finally, his mortal dross burned up. At the end of Seneca's play, the ghost of Hercules appears briefly to Alcmena, his mother, and announces that he has been taken to heaven and deified.

Throughout the last pages of Seneca's play, the chorus comments sympathetically on Hercules' life and end. They remind the reader of Hercules' labours. But they are worried. With Hercules gone, will the gods send other undefeatable monsters? 'To thee, father of all, in wretchedness we pray; let no dread beast be born, no pest; from the fear of savage kings keep this poor world free', they pray to Jupiter. 'If some dread thing again should come to earth, oh, give to forsaken earth a champion.'[16]

Hercules was important to the Romans because he straddled the worlds of gods and men. He had a fully human life, characterised by mistakes, rages, loss, marriage, and children. But, in the end, his human achievements were enough to give him a place among the immortals. The average Roman could not hope to be king; the vast majority of Romans would never see substantial wealth, but they could hope and pray for a glorious life after death, a life that would go on forever, free of all the struggle that takes place below.

Chapter 6

Jason and Medea

You can't really blame modern women for loving Medea. In a sea of sacrificed virgins, sex slaves, and maligned wives, Medea exists to challenge the Roman patriarchy and to chart her own course.

Make no mistake: Medea *is* a clear-cut villain. She commits murder AND infanticide. She betrays her country and her father. Her powers definitely come from the dark side of polytheism. Imagine the forbidden section of the Hogwarts library. Now imagine that Medea somehow got a key and spent most of her childhood there.

The dissonance arises when modern readers come along and think to themselves, 'But she's a teenager!' and then, perhaps, 'Whoa, the goddesses sure did gang up on Medea. It took three of them to bend her will'.

The younger Seneca and Valerius Flaccus both wrote at some length about her. For Seneca, Medea is an inexorable force of nature whose actions were fated from the beginning of time. Flaccus, by contrast, sees the desperate girl, a girl who might have lived and died without scandal or controversy, if she hadn't stumbled on Jason.

And who is this Jason? He is a Greek from Thessaly. He was born to lead, but his father, King Aeson, had been dethroned by his brother, Pelias. Like most usurpers in literature, Pelias was greedy and immoral. This young upstart Jason represented an ongoing threat to his stolen power. Jason's claim to the throne was stronger than Pelias'. Also, Jason was young, strong, even quite handsome!

How do you kill a beautiful young man who is, rather naturally, beloved of everyone who knows him?

Suicide quest!

There was a historic artefact on the other side of the known world that, perhaps technically, belonged to the Thessalians. It was the fleece of a golden ram that was, bizarrely enough, Neptune's offspring. (Because of their descent from the Titans, the Olympians could spawn humans, animals, and monsters, more or less at will. Neptune, in particular, fathered beasts.) After participating in several escapades with a Greek named Phrixus, the ram had been sacrificed to Neptune, who turned the animal's soul into a constellation, making him immortal.

The fleece was treated as a holy object and placed in a grove sacred to Mars. Guarding it was a dragon that never slept. The teeth of this dragon, if planted in the soil like seeds, would grow foot soldiers. The dragon could thus deploy its own army if needed.

Pelias casually told Jason to go fetch this golden fleece. It was a more clever stratagem than you might think. Jason was related to Phrixus, who sacrificed the ram. By the logic of the time, the pelt should have passed to Jason's ownership when Phrixus died.

But the passage to Colchis, the fleece's resting place, was beset with many mortal dangers. If Jason didn't die at sea, the young man would be killed by foreigners, Pelias reasoned. What Pelias did not reckon with was how popular this mission would become and how many champions would attach themselves to it.

The fleece was in the Kingdom of Colchis, occupied by what is modern day Georgia. The trip from Greece to Georgia today takes around thirty hours by car if one drives through Turkey. But our intrepid voyagers crossed the Black Sea in the *Argo*, a ship commissioned by Minerva and built under her careful supervision.

Hercules was the first man to volunteer for the voyage which would come to be called 'The Argonautica'. A young man named Hylas joined him, ostensibly to carry Hercules' weapons, but mostly because our hero enjoyed the boy's company. Flaccus notes that Hylas was quite young, and his hands were not big enough to carry Hercules' club.

The quest for the golden fleece gathered together many other heroes from Roman mythology: Orpheus, the musician; Theseus, the serial husband; Mopsus, skilled in prophecy; and Telamon and Polyphemus, a mortal with the same name as the cyclops, confusingly. The men gathered for a feast the night before they set sail, and they made sacrifices, asking the gods for a smooth journey. They took off in the morning, and the singer/songwriter Orpheus played his lyre and sang their oars into a smooth rhythm so that they didn't clash against each other.

When the *Argo* had passed beyond the horizon, Pelias turned to the second phase of his plan: murder the rest of Jason's family. Fearing that they would be tortured, Aeson and his wife committed suicide by drinking a bowl of poisoned bull's blood. Their infant son was subsequently mutilated and killed by Pelias' men. The gods prevented Jason from learning of his family's destruction, as they feared that sadness would prevent him from completing his mission.

The first stop of the *Argo* was Lemnos, an island kingdom that was dear to Vulcan for very specific reasons. You will remember that the Dei Consentes are one big, blended family. In Lemnos' backstory, Jupiter and Juno quarrelled one day, and Jupiter shackled her and hung her upside down. She was basically suspended in outer space.

Vulcan saw his dear mother held captive and tried to liberate her. Jupiter caught him in the act and angrily pushed him out of heaven. His fall to earth gave him the permanent leg injury for which he is famous.

Vulcan landed on Lemnos. There, the surprised inhabitants recognised him and nursed the god back to health. The care of the Lemnos inhabitants endeared them to the god. In their turn, these islanders honoured Vulcan with prayers and sacrifices, long after he had returned to his forge..

Unfortunately, they did not do the same for Venus, Vulcan's wife. Venus' shrines were neglected throughout Lemnos because the residents identified with Vulcan's rage over her affair with Mars. It is important to note that the islanders committed no open blasphemy. But their best devotion was saved for Vulcan. Venus came to resent the men of Lemnos over the disrespect they showed her. And the Venus of the Argonauts was not a nice lady.

The Argonauts found Lemnos inhabited only by women, which was quite odd. The women had a plausible explanation, though: their husbands were off, pillaging somewhere. This would have been a good time for the Argonauts to inquire where the male children were. They did not

In fact, the women of Lemnos were hiding a terrible secret. Their men had recently returned home from a successful conquest. Their ships were loaded down with treasure and slaves. These Lemnians had *not* betrayed their wives with their captives. They fully intended to hand the female slaves over to their wives as gifts and domestic help.

Venus had no use for this kind of honesty, however. Anxious only to get her revenge, she deployed the goddess, Rumour, a dangerous street god, neither of heaven nor hell, but confined to the human realm, because who but humans need gossip?

Rumour hit the ground running, disguised herself as needed, and convinced the Lemnian women that their husbands were returning home with captive sex slaves. 'They are much more beautiful than you, they will replace you as wives, exile you, then kill your children', was more or less how Rumour incited the women of Lemnos.

The Lemnians couldn't know for sure that Rumour was lying. Replacing all your wives with more exotic, tattooed girls was exactly the kind of thing a band of men from a remote island *could* get away with.

What Rumour was saying sounded wrong, of course, and there would have been doubters. The wives might have summoned their better judgement, eventually. But Venus was playing to win. She descended to Lemnos herself, by night, and burst into house after house, with a severed man's head in her hand. It was still pulsing out its apparent lifeblood onto her skin and garment. In so doing, she activated a bloodthirsty mob.

So the wives of Lemnos killed their husbands, then their fathers, brothers, and sons, to keep them from taking revenge at a later date. The men had weapons, of course, but the women had the element of surprise, and Venus deceived the men by making their wives suddenly seem much larger than they were in real life.

Several husbands ran into a fire to avoid these giants. Princess Hypsipyle, alone, had saved her father, the Lemnian king, by hiding him at the shrine of Bacchus. In the absence of any other rulers, she then took up the position of queen.

How much time passed for the murdering wives before the *Argo* arrived on those bloodied shores? It might have been the next day. A priestess saw the ships making their way to Lemnos, and she delivered a long monologue about the obvious – they had killed all their farmers and fighters; maybe take these sailors to bed and make some more humans.

Where the women are both beautiful and willing, men have been known to forget their mission. It was also the start of the rainy season, the most dangerous for sailors. So most of the Argonauts paired up and enjoyed a long hiatus of physical pleasure.

Hercules, by contrast, stayed on the ship with his mind fixed on the voyage and its goal. Who knows how long the Argonauts might have stayed on Lemnos, otherwise? Might the suicide mission have been abandoned? Instead of Argonauts, might the crew have become the founders of a new Lemnos?

Hercules was praised for his daring, not his patience. When a few days or weeks had passed, he gathered the crew together for a round of insults and shaming. 'This is what you left home for? Where is your ambition? I only joined this mission because it was a heroic opportunity', and finally, 'You mock the prayers of your mothers and fathers who are, probably as we speak, imploring the gods for your success and safe homecoming' was more or less how he coached them.

Luckily, there had been a fair wind for days, so he got no argument. They packed up and returned to the *Argo*, Hipsipyle weeping and tossing gifts at Jason. She begged him to return to her, when he had the fleece. But he made her no promises that he would never keep. In that sense, only, she was luckier than his next girlfriend would be.

Passing a bleak shore on which funeral pyres had been erected, the Argonauts heard a woman's voice calling for help. Finally they spotted Hesione chained to some rocks. From quite a distance, she hollered that she had been left there as a sacrifice.

Neptune had sent a sea monster to punish the people of King Laomedon, and virgin daughters were being offered to placate the beast. Hesione was the daughter of Laomedon. A prophecy said that she would be rescued from certain death by Hercules. And here he was!

Suddenly, they all heard a roar, and the dragon rose out of the sea, swiftly approaching Hercules. Our hero shot a cloud of arrows at it, but none of them even injured the monster. He then dived into the ocean and picked up a giant rock with which to bash the dragon. When it was stunned and down, he killed it with his club, and it sank beneath the waves. No sooner had the dragon disappeared than several shepherds appeared from behind the rocks where they had hidden.

Laomedon, his wife, and son came out of hiding as well, and Laomedon regretted that he could not reward Hercules with a gift of the country's famed horses. The king was not speaking from his heart, however; he was treacherously thinking he would like to murder Hercules in his sleep and steal his weapons. He would not get the chance, though. Hercules made his excuses, explaining that the Argonauts were on serious business, and they cast off.

Juno and Minerva both kept a close eye on the *Argo*'s progress throughout its voyage and homecoming. But they had different motives. Minerva was in it for the high jinks, and Juno was in it because she hated Hercules. Her loyalties would shift later in the story.

When the crew landed in Mysea, Juno found yet another way to do mischief. She looked up at the pine forest hills and spotted some hunting nymphs in short skirts and green armlets, carrying light bows. Dryope was among them.

The goddess of marriage slid quietly down from heaven and leaned up against a dark pine trunk to put a word in Dryope's ear. 'The man I have chosen as your husband is here – on this island', Juno told the nymph. 'He is just as handsome as Bacchus!'

Then, not trusting entirely to Dryope's romantic instincts, Juno sent a stag running through the woods right past Hylas, who gave chase. The deer led the boy around trees and over rocks, letting him get close, but not quite close enough to hit it with an arrow. Finally, the deer leapt over a spring, and Hylas, exhausted, fell down next to the stream and cooled himself off. He didn't see the nymph approaching him until she was upon him with a bear hug that pulled him, inexorably, into her world. He was never seen again. Let us hope that their immortal union was a happy one.

Hercules was surprised not to see his young companion at dinner. A terrible foreboding set in, and he rushed into the woods, calling Hylas' name, but what a god – even a mere nymph – has hidden, no mere mortal shall ever find.

Hercules refused to leave without Hylas. Polyphemus refused to leave without Hercules. Jason cried over the loss, but his crew prevailed on him. The *Argo* set sail, down three crew members. Hercules would, of course, make his way back to Tyrins, eventually, and complete his twelve labours.

The Argonauts had several more adventures before reaching Colchis and the golden fleece. They met up with some old friends. Then, in a weird case of mistaken identity, the Argonauts ended up in battle with them. They saved the blind prophet, Phineus, from a band of harpies. They encountered and overcame a powerful king, famous for killing all his guests. But perhaps the most terrifying challenge was the clashing rocks, giant moving boulders.

These rocks had ground up many ships and left the crews to drown. They churned up a perpetual storm. But, with Hercules off the ship, Juno joined forces with Minerva. Together they jumped down from heaven, each landing on one of the clashing rocks and stilled them forever. The *Argo* sailed between them unharmed and made safe harbour in Colchis.

It was only a matter of time before Jason ran into Medea in the woods. She was with her entourage of maidens, but there was no mistaking the princess in the group. In approaching her, Jason used a very old line from the classics: 'If you are a goddess . . .'[1]

The Greeks always hoped for hospitality, and they invented gods that demanded hospitality. But hospitality is not something you can warrant, it's something you hope for. And the further one gets from Athens, the less constrained civilizations feel by Athenian rules. So when Medea gave Jason directions to her father's palace, she was expecting him to be killed rather quickly. Sharing with foreigners was not the local custom.

At this point in her life, Medea was a very young woman, known to be a magician, yes, but only locally. I like to think of her as 17, but she might have been younger. She was a beauty and a follower of Hecate, a powerful goddess of the underworld. She was also the niece of the powerful witch Circe, who becomes important in Ulysses' story.

Medea was engaged to an Albanian prince who would add a powerful connection to her royal family. She had accepted the engagement as a done deal. She was a loving, obedient, and loyal daughter to her parents. There was no particular reason to think she would become a disrupter.

Despite her association with Hecate, Flaccus portrays Medea as a good-natured girl who knows how to regulate her emotions. She prays often, and her prayers are mostly for the ongoing welfare of others. She obeys her mother and father and cares diligently for her pet dragon.

Flaccus' version of the *Argonautica* has often been dismissed as clumsy, not as artistic as the work of Apollonius of Rhodes who also took up the subject in the Greek language. But Flaccus' depiction of a perfectly healthy girl descending into complete and utter madness is unmatched anywhere in literature.

Jason was sea-battered and exhausted, not just from his voyage, but also from anxiety. He had lost some of his youthful good looks, but Juno used her powers to restore his beauty and make him dazzle. She hid him in a cloud until he reached the centre of town and the temple where Aeetes, King of Colchis, was making sacrifices to the sun god, who happened to be Aeetes' father.

Aeetes' parents were both immortals. Despite that rather illustrious heritage, he was not a noble man. He had no intention of handing over the fleece, but he did see an opportunity to use Jason and his crew. Somehow, Aeetes convinced the Argonauts to join him in fighting against his brother Perses. Perses, Aeetes assured the Argonauts, was trying to usurp the throne. This was a vile deception.

The truth was that Perses had already told Aeetes to hand the fleece over to the Thessalians. It belonged to them, for gods' sake, Perses noted. Phryxus was Greek. Jason was his heir. A priest had also told Aeetes that it was the will of the gods that Jason win the ramskin. That was what Perses and Aeetes were really quarrelling about.

But the Argonauts did not know that. Aeetes told them, sure, he would give them the fleece, but first he needed them to join him in battle against his usurping brother. The Argonauts agreed. Perses got wind that the Argonauts had chosen Aeetes' side, and he tried to send them a message, setting them straight. But Mars wanted a war, so he set up a loud war cry that infected the fighters and drove them immediately into battle.

Meanwhile, Juno had decided to support Jason and the Argonauts against the Colchians, now that Hercules was not one of their number. And, like most narcissists, she didn't care who she destroyed in the process of getting her way. She took the form of Medea's sister, Chalciope, and strode to Medea's chamber.

In the guise of Chalciope, Juno persuaded Medea to climb to the top of the city wall and watch the battle. The girl had already seen Jason without losing her head. But now she was under the influence of the most powerful Olympian goddess, one whose largely-unused skill set was creating harmonious human pairings.

Medea saw Jason running here and there on the battlefield, agile, strong, efficient. He was an able fighter, but Juno increased his strength and ability so that Medea could not help but admire him. Loyal sister and Colchian that Medea was, she looked for her brother, Absyrtus, and her fiancé, Stygus. But everywhere she looked, there was Jason.

She wondered, briefly, if the woman sitting with her was really her sister. But then she did start feeling some empathy for the Greek visitors. She wondered out loud if her father would play fair and give up the fleece as he had promised. And why were the Argonauts fighting for a country that was foreign to them? When she heard these questions, Juno believed that she had won, and Medea would take Jason's part in everything.

She was wrong. Medea was much stronger than Juno thought.

With the help of the Argonauts, Aeetes won the battle against his brother. The Argonauts were anxious to collect the fleece and be off. While they waited for Aeetes to complete his morning sacrifices, Jason looked around for the artefact. Surely, they had brought it from the sacred grove so that it would be ready to go aboard the *Argo*.

When he finally addressed the Argonauts, Aeetes acted like he had never met them. He had never heard of Greece. They must be pirates. Crazy pirates. He ordered them to leave. Or if they still wanted the fleece, they would have to subdue some magic bulls on the plain of Mars, and use them to plough and plant some seeds.

Jason could now see that he was dealing with another tyrant, much like the uncle back in Thessaly. It was a bitter realisation. In despair, he swore that he would never leave Colchis without the fleece. So he agreed to the new challenge, even though it spelled certain death.

Medea's fledgling passion had kept her awake for much of the night, but she applied reason and logic to the situation. It was 'madness' to be thinking of Jason, definitely a mistake, she explained to herself. Her father should just give him the fleece, and let him leave. Upon awaking, she revisited this passion and found that she could get the better of it.

As she said her morning prayers, she begged the gods to let Jason return safely to Greece. Touchingly, she added a prayer that he would not hate her father. Crush, done and dusted. She had shaken off most of Juno's poison and regained possession of her virgin heart.

Juno saw that the girl had walked herself back into a self-regulated condition. So she pulled out the big guns. She flew to Venus and complained that Medea had stubbornly eluded madness and delusion. It would take a LOT of courage for a girl brought up like she was to leave her father's house and run away with a foreigner. A moment's admiration of Jason was not going to accomplish that. She needed that mad, crazy, reckless kind of love. The kind the poets write about.

Venus agreed to help. In order to deceive Medea effectively, she took the form of Circe, Medea's powerful aunt, a minor goddess in her own right. Circe had left Colchis long before, and Medea did not recognise her at first when the disguised goddess appeared in her chambers. The girl assumed that Circe could travel, using magic, so she was only briefly surprised to see her.

Venus' presence alone was enough to disturb Medea's tranquillity, and her thoughts returned chaotically to Jason. As Circe, Venus implied that Medea was too good to marry any Colchians. Medea assured her aunt that she would never be 'driven' into a marriage she didn't want. Her alliance with Hecate guaranteed that.

Medea begged Circe to give her a sleeping potion. The infatuation was wrecking her, and she needed sleep to restore her sanity. Venus could not have been less interested in helping Medea recover her mental health. Instead, she took the girl in her arms and put the seal on her desire. She had met Jason, Venus claimed, and he had asked her to take this message to Medea: 'Please save us'.

He had nothing to pay her, but he offered himself. Circe could have become his champion, but she already had so much glory! Now it was Medea's turn to shine, Venus-as-Circe explained.

It would take a lot of nerve for a well-off 17-year-old to leave her safe home, where there was always food on the table. Even more courage would be required to jump on a motorless kayak and travel the seas with an all-male crew. Medea definitely knew better. She was still fighting with the gods for control of her emotions; 'she felt that she was being utterly vanquished by some strange power'.[2] She considered a noble suicide. It would be better than betraying her father and country, as she must do to help Jason, she reasoned.

She felt a sudden, huge surge of anger against her aunt. It was so violent, she could barely keep herself from throttling the disguised goddess. She started shaking, and looking for someplace to hide, an escape hatch. There was nowhere to go. She would have to see this adventure through. She had a brief premonition of the future crimes she would commit.

Medea workshopped her magic, praying to Hecate for a power surge, and isolating a powerful herb from the Caucasus. This plant drew its magic directly from the titan Prometheus. It grew in soil nourished by droppings from the giant's liver. These deposits occurred as the vulture pecked away at him.

Around this time, Juno sent the rainbow goddess, Iris, to ensure that Jason would get to a secret meeting with Medea. At that rendezvous, Medea explained that she would help the Argonauts, but she would need protection from her father afterward. Jason was in no position to bargain; desperately, he seized on her help and made the kind of promises you should keep – especially to a powerful woman destined for immortality.

To modern readers, his marriage proposal looks reckless and glib, like the pitch of a used car salesman. But Medea, too, was in an inescapable predicament. She accepted his impromptu promise to make her his wife.

Jason vowed that he would never forget her help. If he should ever be ungrateful, 'then let thy flames and cunning arts afright me', he swore.[3] A nearby Fury, who had seen Medea's future, happened to hear that and pledged to punish Jason when he broke that promise. Having chosen a side, finally, Medea got to work and put enchantments on Jason's body, his spear, and shield to protect him in the coming conflict. She gave him an enchanted helmet, and told him when to throw it into the crowd.

Morning found Jason as ready to tame Aeetes' wild bulls as he would ever be. Aeetes had expected the Argonauts to flee in the night. So he was surprised to learn that the Thessalian was already on the field of battle, armed and ready.

Colchians and Argonauts all gathered on the plains to watch the spectacle. The bulls were clearly supernatural. They had never been yoked to a plough, and they shot flames from their bronze mouths and hooves. One of them wasted no time charging Jason. Souped up with Medea's enchantments, he grabbed them, one at a time, by the horns and pushed them under the yokes. Once they were hooked up to ploughs, Jason scattered a supply of 'seeds' on the ground as he had been commanded to do by Aeetes.

Because Medea was helping him, Jason knew these were not real seeds, but dragon's teeth. They sprouted immediately and a race of warlike men, in full battle armour, arose from the earth like fast-growing trees. Jason threw the enchanted helmet into their midst, as Medea had directed him to do. The lobbed helmet was an act of war, and the new men immediately started killing each other. Before Aeetes could issue any orders, the earth opened and swallowed the entire army of dragon-teeth fighters.

Jason and Medea met at Mars' grove, guarded by a very serpentine dragon who encircled the fleece. At this point in Flaccus' *Argonautica*, it emerges that the dragon is Medea's pet, possibly her familiar. She is the only one who feeds him, and the two even snuggle together.

Using sedatives of her own concoction, she put the beast into a sound slumber while Jason collected the fleece. The reader with pets will feel her heart breaking as Medea prays that her beloved dragon will forget her and find another grove to live in, now that his sacred watch is done.

By prior arrangement, Jason and Medea met the other Argonauts at a river mouth. When his crew caught a glimpse of the radiant fleece in the distance, they cheered. The Greeks wasted no time putting distance between the Argo and Colchis, but the voice of Medea's mother, Idyia, and her sister and handmaidens assailed them while they were furiously rowing.

Idyia wanted her daughter back, she screamed. The Greeks could have the fleece. Why didn't Medea say she wanted to marry Jason? They would have allowed it! The queen was so distraught that she imagined abandoning the rest of her family and travelling with the Argonauts. Why had Medea not taken her mother into her confidence? They could be on the boat together now, seeing the world.

'Turn the boat around', the mournful, disembodied voice shrieked, and then, revealing that she *had* taken her daughter's true measure, she added, 'I know you can'.[4]

The wedding took place on the island of Peuce. Both Jason and Medea were at the height of their beauty, the crew acted as bridal party and guests. Pollux handled the sacred fire and water. But there were no good omens. The fire did not blaze. There was a prophet – Mopsus – among the Argonauts, but he foresaw only a brief period of love for the newlyweds. Whether he told the assembled guests that or kept it to himself, Flaccus does not tell us.[5]

Medea did not get away from Colchis scot-free. Her brother, Absyrtus, and her fiancé, Styrus, angrily pursued the *Argo* with Styrus raging about his stolen property. Whether Medea had consented to run away or not was of no importance to him. Jason had stolen his 'dowry', he complained. He was talking about the fleece, not his fiancée.

In almost no time, the *Argo* crew were arguing about whether they should really have a girl on this voyage and whether they should give her back to the Colchians. Absyrtus' ship was wrecked in a storm, and the Greeks escaped them, but Medea could see a change in Jason's attitude toward her. The last we see of her in Flaccus' *Argonautica*, she is joking bitterly about whether her marriage will survive until they reach Thessaly.

We pick up the story in Hyginus' *Fabulae*. When they were nearing Jason's home island of Iolcus, Medea and Jason discussed whether to kill Pelias, and Medea declared that she would do it. To that end, she entered Pelias' palace, alone, disguised as one of his daughters. She found her 'sisters' and convinced them that she could de-age their father. To illustrate, she put an old ram into a giant cooking pot and out jumped a baby goat.

All the sisters had to do was kill their father and put his body in the same cauldron, Medea explained. The sisters did as instructed. Pelias, however, did not revive. His daughters soon apprehended that they had killed him. With Pelias dead, Jason returned victoriously to Iolcus without fear of reprisal. He awarded governorship of the city to Acastus, Pelias' son, who had followed Jason to Colchis.[6]

Medea and Jason then fled to Corinth where they found sanctuary under King Creon. The two lived in relative happiness for ten years. At least, we know of no scandal attached to them during this time. They had two sons. But, according to Hyginus, Jason never got over his embarrassment at having a 'foreign' wife.

Yes, there was gossip about Medea. She was never going to fit in or be a regular princess. Was it her wrong-colour clothes or weird jewellery or facial piercings or tattoos? Or was it the fact that she could never fully disguise her power?

Back in Iolcus, Acastus got around to resenting the death of his father. Though Medea and Jason had lived relatively quiet lives, Creon got word that Acastus wanted revenge. Creon had to protect his kingdom from a needless war, but he was also under some obligation to protect Jason.

The hero of the golden fleece adventure had become famous all over the known world. Luckily, Creon had a daughter whom he could now offer in marriage to the hero of the Argonautica. This arrangement was clearly meant to cut Medea out of the family picture.

For Medea, Creon made no provision. She begged him for custody of her children. He declared that he would raise them as his own. She begged him to give her a small corner of his kingdom to live quietly. He declined and exiled her under a tight deadline. She was a known criminal who had betrayed her own country and killed Pelias. She had no political capital in Corinth.

Medea is most famous for killing her own children. I implore you, dear reader, not to mistake anything I write for excusing that act. But who was Medea, really? What was she? According to some sources, she was a goddess. Her aunt, Circe, was a goddess, and her parents were the same divinities that Medea called grandmother and grandfather. Flaccus portrays her as a mortal girl caught up in events beyond her control. The ancient vase painters, however, thought she was a goddess and painted her as such. For Seneca, the Younger, she was a contradiction, a child killer who is also divinely rescued from any consequences of her actions.

Seneca's Medea took her exile more as an insult than an injury. She ruminated, not on where she would go, but on how she would punish those who rejected her.

She also sensed that a transformation was at hand. She was evolving from a dreamy girl to a powerful witch. She had, technically, already committed murder by getting Pelias' daughters to kill their father. But that was an act of girlhood; she could see that fulfilling her potential required a bigger act of violence. This coming murder spree would show who she really was.

In a last conversation with his wife, while the music for his wedding to another woman was playing in the background, Jason told Medea that he was doing this for their children. She asked him, for the last time, to run away with her *as she had run with him*. He refused. He was genuinely frightened of Creon and Acastus.

He should have been frightened of his wife.

Medea then sent her two sons to Creusa, Creon's daughter and Jason's fiancée, with 'wedding gifts'. These turned out to be a poisoned robe, a gold necklace, and a gold band which Medea had poisoned with hidden fire. She had taken this magic fire directly from Prometheus, the titan doomed to have his liver pecked, who had been her tutor, according to Seneca. She also received flames as a gift from her cousin, Phaeton.[7]

Once she had put on these poisoned gifts, Creusa burst into flames, along with her father, Creon, who tried to help her. The fire then quickly spread to the rest of the residence. When Jason found Medea, she was holding their son, and she slit his throat right in front of the boy's father.

She fled to the roof with her remaining child, the question of her mortality literally still hanging in the air. The fire spread to the neighbourhood. Jason ordered his men to destroy the house that his wife was standing on. In answer, she killed his other son. A chariot appeared from heaven moving on its own power, landed on the roof, and whisked her away from the crime scene.[8]

So . . . goddess, then. Your humble author could find no record of her death in the Roman sources. Jason is last seen at the Calydonian boar hunt in the *Metamorphoses*. According to the Greeks, he died while sleeping under the *Argo*. A piece of the old, rotting ship fell down and killed him; it was an inglorious death for such a high-spirited, voyaging hero.

Medea settled in Athens, where she married Aegeus. The two had a son named Medus. Eventually, a priestess of Diana complained to Aegeus that Medea's crimes were polluting the temple sacrifices. So, Medea was banished again. Not a problem, though, because somewhere in her many adventures, she had acquired two winged dragons who were trained to pull chariots. She hitched up these beasts and flew back to Colchis, land of her birth.

On the way, she landed on the island where her brother, Absyrtus, had died, after pursuing the fleece and being shipwrecked. His entire crew had been afraid to go home without the fleece. So they settled the island and, in honour of Absyrtus, they named it Absoris.

The settlers of that island were overrun by snakes. Using her magic, Medea gathered them up and imprisoned them in her brother's grave. She also rendered them immortal, so long as they stayed in their prison. If they left, they would die of old age.[9]

The woman who returned to Colchis was not the same girl who left it in tears, terrified of her father, torn apart by passion for a foreigner. Formerly, she had used magic sparingly and with a healthy fear of its dangers. As a grown woman, she used it calculatedly.

The Roman writers left her on Colchis. Did she live a long life on the island of her birth, at the edge of the known world? Did she die, content with her choices, perhaps surrounded with grandchildren? Her actions will always horrify us – at the same time that we wonder at her courage and power. Her subsequent life, though, is mostly a blank. The poets are done with her.

PART III

THE TROJAN WAR

Preamble

You might say that the Trojan War began when Jupiter saw Leda, another beautiful mortal that he must seduce. He took the form of a swan to make love to her. Whether this was a rape or a fling depends on what artist you wish to believe. The ancient poets left a lot to the imagination, and that was a field day for vase painters. A late classical vase painting owned by the Paul Getty Museum in Malibu shows Leda kissing the swan on the beak with both her hands caressing his head and neck. It definitely looks consensual.

In William Butler Yeats' poem 'Leda and the Swan', it's definitely a rape, and he draws a straight line between that violence and the burning and sacking of Troy. He writes:

> A shudder in the loins engenders there
> The broken wall, the burning roof and tower
> And Agamemnon dead.[1]

But Yeats does not feel sorry for Leda. He ruminates on whether she picked up any of Jupiter's 'knowledge and power' before he dropped her from his beak. There's an element of envy on the poet's part.

If you follow that envy, you can see Jupiter as the force of artistic inspiration and Leda as the artist/poet who waits and longs for a momentary glimpse of the immortal realm, a visit from a god, if you will. When I speak of inspiration, I'm talking about the world we cannot see with ordinary eyes. Poets value that inspiration. That's why they invented the muses, goddesses of creativity.

Leda, who was a queen of Sparta, had sex with her husband, Tyndareus, on the same day as her encounter with Jupiter. Nine months later, she gave birth to four infants. Two were boys, Castor and Pollux. As adults, they would both fight in the Trojan war.

The other two babies, Helen and Clytemnestra, were girls, and you could say that they functioned as bookends for the Trojan War, Helen at the beginning and Clytemnestra at the end. Helen and Pollux were the semi-divine children of Jupiter. He would, of course, have great courage and strength. She would be a great beauty, too great. No one needs to be that beautiful.

Or you might prefer to believe that the war began in the Garden of the Hesperides. This magical garden setting was where Paris judged the beauty of the most powerful goddesses in the world. But why was there a contest, and why would goddesses care about Paris' opinion? Read on.

The goddess of discord had not been invited to the wedding of Peleus and Thetis. Who wants discord at a wedding? But, on this occasion she felt snubbed, so she crashed the party anyway. She threw a golden apple into the centre of the feast. It was inscribed with the words, 'for the most beautiful'.

To whom should this apple belong? Let the discord begin.

You might think that Venus would, automatically, win in any beauty contest, but the other goddesses did *not* consider that a given. Both Juno and Minerva thought the apple should belong to them. Of course, beauty is both subjective and subject to context. As an older woman, in a long, long marriage, I now imagine Jupiter telling Juno, 'Darling, of course you're the most beautiful', and Vulcan telling Venus, 'Hey Gorgeous, they have nothing on you', and then Jupiter telling his daughter Minerva, 'Darling, of course you're the most beautiful'.

At any rate, the goddesses quarrelled, very unbecomingly, over this issue. Eventually, they decided on a third-party adjudicator. Paris may have been chosen because of his unorthodox upbringing as a shepherd. More on that later.

The Victorian poet, Alfred Tennyson, found the judgement of Paris fascinating. He reinvented the judgement. Instead of a beauty contest, it is a test of Paris' character as seen through the eyes of Oenone, a river goddess and Paris' lover. In Tennyson's poem, Oenone sings a prayer to the goddess

Ida in which she recounts watching the judgement in hiding from a distance. She saw her lover approach: 'Beautiful Paris, evil-hearted Paris'.

She ran to him, and he showed her the golden apple. Clearly, it was intended for the most beautiful female in the universe. And he was the one elected to decide! he bragged. He told Oenone to hide in a nearby cave so she could spy on the proceedings.

First came Juno. A peacock landed ahead of her. It was her symbol. Brazenly, she offered Paris money and political power: 'Honour', she said, 'and homage, tax and toll'. Paris was tempted.

Minerva stood at a distance, her arms and legs bared and holding her spear. She had no intention of flirting with Paris, but she launched into her monologue. Self-knowledge and self-discipline were the gifts she offered, along with the ability to judge right from wrong and choose right, no matter the cost.

It really doesn't sound that appealing. But somehow Oenone knew that Minerva – whose other name was Pallas – was the right choice. (The reader knows he should have given it to Oenone.)

> I cried, 'O Paris,
> Give it to Pallas!' but he heard me not,
> Or hearing would not hear me, woe is me!

Before Paris had time to seriously consider a life of self-denial, Venus got his attention. Really, there was no ignoring her.

> Idalian Aphroditè [the Greek name for Venus] beautiful,
> Fresh as the foam, new-bathed in Paphian wells,
> With rosy slender fingers backward drew
> From her warm brows and bosom her deep hair
> Ambrosial, golden round her lucid throat
> And shoulder.

If that weren't enough, she leaned in and whispered in Paris' ear:

> 'I promise thee
> The fairest and most loving wife in Greece.'

Paris gave the apple to Venus, of course, and the goddess arranged for him to kidnap Helen away from her husband and kingdom. He had told Oenone a thousand times that she was beautiful while she held him tightly in her arms. Abandoned, Oenone closed her song by saying that she would now be alone the rest of her life.[2]

Did Helen fall in love with Paris, or did he take her by force? And, if by force, then why would he need to bribe Venus? Equally, if she fell for him, why would he need to bribe Venus? (Paris does make Hyginus' list of exceptionally attractive men.) You must resolve this dilemma in your own imagination, I'm afraid, dear reader.

What your humble author finds interesting is that Helen never suffered. She was happily married to Menelaus, then happily paired up with Paris. She bore children to both of them. When Troy was ravaged, and the Trojan widows were screaming their sorrows on the butchered battlefield, Helen was sailing back to Sparta with her husband, King Menelaus. She lived with him in his palace to the end of her days, played hostess, and it appears that everyone in their circle, servants included, was under orders never to mention (ahem, sh!) the Trojan Incident of ten years duration.

Sorry for the spoiler, but the thought of Helen, standing on the battlements of Troy looking down at her Greek husband and his entire army while Greeks and Trojans *that she knew by name* killed each other, is so worth it.

The Fleet

When Christopher Marlowe wrote that Helen's face 'launched a thousand ships', he might have been exaggerating. But he was faithful to his sources. Ovid and Seneca agreed that the Greeks assembled a fleet that size. Hyginus came up with a more realistic number: 245 ships.[3]

Menelaus was the king of Sparta and Helen's cuckolded husband, so of course his resources were deployed. His elder brother Agamemnon, king of Mycenae, lent his armies and ships. Between them, Agamemnon and Menelaus brought 160 ships to the war effort. By consensus, Agamemnon took the lead over the combined Greek forces.

Among the other volunteers in the Greek camp were Ulysses, Diomedes, Patroclus, Nestor, Achilles, Achilles' son Neoptolemus, and two men named Ajax. The list of Greek fighters who went to Troy overlaps considerably with the list of Helen's acknowledged former suitors. That list was so long that Hyginus needed to give us the complete roster in his *Fabulae*.[4] It includes Ulysses, Diomedes, Patroclus, and both the Ajaxes.

Notably absent from the list of suitors was Paris, who was raised as an abandoned orphan far outside his father, Priam's, palace. During his gestation, his mother, Queen Hecuba, had dreamt that she gave birth to a torch, and from that torch came numerous serpents. It was a troubling nightmare, and obviously a premonition about the downfall of Troy, which this baby would, eventually, bring about.

Having heard her dream, several soothsayers told Hecuba that she should kill the baby at birth. Hecuba did not have the heart to do that with her own hands. So she assigned servants to kill the baby. They didn't have the heart to kill a baby either. Instead, they did as servants in mythology had done before. They left Paris on a rock or in a field to die of exposure to weather and wildlife, and so he was rescued and raised by shepherds.

As an adult, or at least a teenager, Paris had a bull that he was quite fond of. One day, Priam's men took his bull to be a prize at King Priam's upcoming games. Ironically, these games were held in honour of Priam's lost son, Paris. To that end, Priam had sent men to look for the finest bull in the region. And that happened to be the still-living Paris' pet.

Paris did not accept the loss of his bull sitting down. He showed up at the games, won every round, and took his bull back. Priam's other sons competed, so Paris had to win against many men to whom he was unknowingly related.

One of these siblings, Deiphobus, resented Paris' success. He let his temper get the better of him and attacked. The shepherd quickly sought the protection of Jupiter's shrine, where convention said he could not be killed or hurt without severely offending the gods. At this point, Cassandra, who was given the gift of insight, recognised Paris as her brother and Deiphobus'. Priam believed her, and Paris was reintroduced into the royal Trojan family – at his own memorial.

So Paris was not among Helen's original suitors. Nor was he part of the formal accord made after she married. When Menelaus became

Helen's husband, the other suitors made a pact among themselves that they would defend and protect Menelaus' marriage. The true purpose of the pact was to guarantee that none of the former suitors would storm Menelaus' palace and take her as a sex slave, of course. Before her marriage, even, the Greeks were already worried that her extreme beauty would get Helen kidnapped.

Not everyone who swore to the pact was thrilled with the notion of going to war, though. Ulysses may have wanted Helen at some point in his life, but that was years ago! Since then, he had married Penelope, who proved a prize throughout their marriage. And she had just given birth to a baby boy.

If that were not enough to turn him into a peacemonger, he had also heard a disturbing prophecy. This prophecy warned Ulysses that, if he went to Troy, it would take him twenty years to get back to Ithaca, of which he was king. And he would return utterly destitute and alone, all his men killed or lost. Prophecies always come true in the ancient Roman stories. And there is no evading your destiny.

Agamemnon, Menelaus, and Palamedes formed a diplomatic mission, sailing to Ithaca to recruit him. Ulysses saw them coming. He knew what they were there for, and he had a plan. He would enact 'the crazy farmer who is of no use to anyone'.

He tethered a bull and horse together to a plough and let them yank the plough in circles with their different sizes. To add to the appearance of madness, he put on a funny hat that Hyginus simply describes as 'felt'. (Something definitely lost in translation there.) Palamedes saw through the ruse, but he did not graciously let Ulysses off the hook. Instead, he grabbed Penelope's baby, Telemachus, out of his cradle and set him in front of the plough with the words, 'Put aside your trickery and join the others bound by oath'.[5]

When he saw his son in danger from a runaway plough, Ulysses dropped the act immediately, saved his kid, and agreed to bring his twelve ships along with fighters from Ithaca. But he neither forgot nor forgave Palamedes for exposing him. The man had effectively separated him from his homeland and wife for the next twenty years.

Ulysses, in his turn, tricked the great Achilles into joining the war effort. Achilles was the son of King Peleus of the Myrmidons and Thetis, a powerful sea goddess. Thetis was a strikingly beautiful nereid, and, prior to her marriage, she attracted the lust of both Jupiter and Neptune.

But those powerful gods heard a prophecy that Thetis would bear a son greater in strength and skill than his father. That was enough to give them pause. The divine brothers decided that Thetis should marry a mortal king, and then it would be okay if her son were greater. It was at that wedding between Thetis and Peleus that Discord threw the golden apple.

By the time the troops were rallied for the Trojan war, the prodigy, Achilles, was grown well into adulthood and a father himself. His mother, Thetis, had heard a prophecy that he would die in the coming war, so she sent him to hide on the island of Scyros. There he was the guest of King Lycomedes.

The Greeks learned where he was, and they sent Ulysses to recruit him. Lycomedes had dressed Achilles up as a girl and placed him in a group of maidens where he blended right in. Ulysses found these girls in a courtyard, and he presented them with a number of gifts, mostly girl stuff, but including a shield and spear.

Then Ulysses ordered one of his men to sound the call to arms on his instrument while other Ithacans smacked their shields and swords together, making a terrible racket that sounded like military troops arriving. Achilles gave himself away by tearing off his dress and picking up a shield and a spear, in immediate preparation for war. From that point, Ulysses was able to cajole him into joining the war effort. Achilles would now have to fulfil both the prophecies concerning him: that he would be greater than his father, and that he would be killed on the field of battle.

Iphigenia

During a storm, the Greek ships docked at Aulis, a fishing village. Thousands of men waited for a propitious wind. They were young, strong, jacked up on testosterone. And they were stuck. This was, potentially, a dangerous mob, and something needed to be done on an emergency basis.

Then, Agamemnon went and killed a deer that was sacred to Diana. The goddess would not let the fleet depart until she had been placated with the blood of a virgin. And that virgin must be Agamemnon's daughter,

Iphigenia, born to him by his wife Clytemnestra. It was Calchas, the travelling priest, who interpreted Diana's will for the fleet. The Greeks put a good deal of stock in Calchas' prophecies.

While at Aulis, the men saw a blue green serpent ascend a tree and eat all eight of the baby chicks who were nesting there. Then he downed the mother bird who had been helplessly trying to save her offspring. Calchas spoke up and interpreted that strange sight. He told the crews they would need nine years to defeat the Trojans, but they would triumph in the end, like the serpent.

The storm off the coast of Aulis raged on, however, and thousands of men – angry, horny, poor impulse control – were still stuck at Aulis. Agamemnon strove briefly with his conscience, but finally agreed to his daughter's sacrifice, having been urged on to it by Ulysses. The needs of the state came before the needs of any young woman to go on living; this much is entirely clear from Roman myth.

I have to confess that, when teaching mythology in translation, I may have used the phrase, 'When in doubt, sacrifice a virgin', at least once a semester, simply because it happens *so* often in the ancient texts, including Norse and Hindu mythologies.

The ancient Romans assigned little value to a young, unmarried woman. She could be murdered as needed. Killing a dinner guest was a crime. Throwing a statue of Jupiter was a crime. Denying sex to a god was a crime. Killing someone you were related to was a crime, as long as it was not a virgin female. But a girl's life was very, very cheap.

Iphigenia came to the altar surrounded by crying attendants. Prayers were chanted, incense burned. According to other sources, the girl was killed, but at the last possible second, Ovid's Diana threw a mist over the proceedings and substituted a deer for Iphigenia. Human sacrifice would not be outlawed in the Roman Republic until a few years after Ovid's death, however.

So Diana whisked Iphigenia away from the altar and spirited her through the clouds to Tauris where she became a priestess and was eventually reunited with her siblings, Orestes and Electra. Clytemnestra believed her daughter was sacrificed and never learned the truth.

In 1977, Greek filmmaker Michael Cacoyannis released a film that tells Iphigenia's story rather brilliantly. Casting Irene Papas as

Clytemnestra, Agamemnon's very angry wife, was genius. Cacoyannis turned the storms into a hot, dry spell, and the ships cannot sail because there is no wind of any kind.

As Iphigenia is led to the altar, the viewer can see the wind picking up in the trees. After her death, as the men sail off to Troy, the look on Clytemnestra's face presages her vengeful murder of Agamemnon.[6] The nine years of the Trojan War and the war's aftermath, in which the heroes fought to return home, were nowhere near enough for her to forget the murder of her daughter.

Chapter 8

The Battlefield and the Horse

You must not forget, dear reader, that this book takes the Roman point of view. Romans believed they were descended from the displaced Trojans, the very ones who sailed off from ruined Troy to find another home. And historians agree that the Trojan immigrants formed at least one part of the early Roman Empire's population.

So Roman poets thought that the Trojans were the true heroes of the war, even though they lost. Simultaneously, the Greeks already had a serious problem with internecine conflict before they ever landed in Troy. They acted out many personal grudges on the battlefield.

If you read Greek sources on the Trojan War, you might conclude that Odysseus was the hero of that conflict. To the Trojans, however, Odysseus was Ulysses, and he is a cheater and deceiver. He always wins, which makes him admirable across the cultures, but he wins in ways that are often underhanded.

The 245 (not a thousand) Greek ships arrived on Troy's beaches. The Trojan warriors were waiting for them. The Greeks had heard a prophecy that the first one of them to set foot on Troy's beach would die. That seems like a safe prophecy – the Trojans would have seen that fleet from at least twenty miles off. They would already have sent their best fighters to meet them. Of course they were going to shoot the first person to get off a boat.

That unfortunate person happened to be Iolaus. (This is not Hercules' nephew; it's a different Iolaus, confusingly enough.) He fell to Hector's first flying arrow. Iolaus' wife, Laodamia, was inconsolable. She prayed so hard to the gods that they could not deny her request – to spend three more hours with her husband. Mercury escorted the dead Iolaus back to the world of the living and, three hours later, escorted him back to Hades.

Laodamia simply could not get over him, though. She created a wax effigy of her late husband, and one day a servant saw her kissing it. Her father thought this behaviour aberrant, so he burned the effigy in a fire. In her anguish, Laodamia threw herself upon the flames and died.

Hector, King Priam's son by his loyal wife Hecuba, soon became the hero and leader of the battle on the Trojan side. Achilles emerged as a great champion on the Greek side, and he fulfilled the prophecy that Jupiter and Neptune were so afraid of.

In Roman sources, Achilles was mostly invulnerable. He was mortal, but he was born of a goddess. His mother dipped him in the River Styx when he was a baby, and the water of that magic river formed a protective barrier over his whole body, except his left heel. Thetis had to hold that heel as she was lowering him.

Ovid has him dashing around the battlefield in a chariot, killing Trojans rather easily. Early in the war, he spotted Neptune's mortal son, Cycnus. Achilles threw his spear at this young man, but it didn't leave a bruise or scratch on the boy who was obviously under the protection of Neptune.

Achilles wondered briefly if his spear tip was lost or blunt, so he threw a test spear at Menoetes who died on the spot. Achilles then struck Cycnus again, but the man could not be wounded with a weapon. Enraged that the gods had given Cycnus an invulnerability similar to his own, the Greek hero jumped on Neptune's son and finally strangled Cycnus with his own helmet strings. Neptune, god of the seas, cherished his son and turned Cycnus into a swan, so that his body could not be dragged behind Achilles' chariot. Though Achilles had done nothing wrong, according to the laws of mythic war, Neptune never forgave him for the death of Cycnus.

One of the most nefarious stories surrounding Ulysses is his revenge on Palamedes. You will remember Palamedes as the man who nearly killed baby Telemachus by putting him on the ground in front of an ox and horse. Ulysses had not forgotten about that. He hatched a rather elaborate plan.

First, he sent a message to Agamemnon saying that, in a dream, the gods had told him they must move camp and do it in one day. Agamemnon chose to believe this dream, and he gave orders to move camp expeditiously. Once the move was completed, Ulysses buried 'a great mass of gold' underneath Palamedes' former camp site.[1]

Then he compelled one of the Trojan captives to take a letter to Priam. This message, written by Ulysses, looked like it was written by Palamedes to King Priam of the Trojans, and it definitely gave the impression that Palamedes was accepting gold to betray his fellow fighters. Just minutes after the Trojan had left camp with the letter, Ulysses sent someone else to kill him.

When the captive's body was discovered with the damning letter, Palamedes denied collaborating with Priam. But when the gold was found under his former camp site, the Greek fighters set on him as a mob and killed him.[2]

The murder of Palamedes would not be the only failure of leadership on the Greek side of the war. Agamemnon was the official leader of the Greek army, but Achilles had stolen the spotlight. He was an amazing fighter, the kind that only comes along once a generation or so. So Agamemnon did what no leader should ever do: he showed the star who is boss.

He commandeered Briseis from out of Achilles' tent. Briseis had been the wife of a prince until the Greeks sacked her city, and Achilles took her as a sex slave. She was desired for her great beauty, but the conflict between Agamemnon and Achilles was more about one upmanship than attraction. When Agamemnon bragged that he would rather sleep with Briseis than with his own wife, he was not setting himself up for future domestic happiness either.

Achilles ceded Briseis to the official war leader, but he was deeply insulted, and he demonstrated his peeve loudly by boycotting the war. For several days, he sat in his tent, playing the cithara, a hand-held harp, and refusing to fight. Patroclus, a dear friend, possibly a lover, showed up in Achilles' tent and reproached him.

Led by Hector, the Trojans were now in ascendance, Patroclus complained. Achilles refused to rejoin the fray, but he gave his armour to Patroclus. Looking in every way like the fierce and unassailable

Achilles, Patroclus went back to the field and took it back for the Greeks, killing the great Sarpedon, son of Europa by Jupiter, in the process. Hector then crossed weapons with Patroclus, thinking he was Achilles, and killed him. The Trojans stripped the Greek champion's armour only to discover that Achilles was not inside it.

Achilles was enraged at the death of Patroclus, and he immediately wished to re-enter the war, but he had no armour. Mad with grief, he determined to go back into combat without that protection. But Thetis would not allow it. With a speed of which only the gods are capable, she found Vulcan and commissioned him to make another suit of armour. Then her fellow nereids spirited it across the seas to Achilles.

With this new armour, Achilles killed Hector, which should have felt like a decisive moment, but the war remained at a stalemate because of the city's supernaturally strong walls. The Greeks definitely had more kills, but they did not and could not win so long as the city remained safe and intact. If they left now, they would return to their homes empty handed; all the treasures of Troy were safe behind the walls and ramparts.

Achilles dragged Hector's dead body around the battlefield behind his chariot to insult the Trojans. It was a needless gesture. The enemy could not have been any more devastated at the death of their prince. This desecration of a corpse, withheld from appropriate rites, was shocking even to the gods who intervened. Under Jupiter's command, Mercury escorted old Priam out to the battlefield where he successfully negotiated to buy his son's body back from the Greeks.

Agamemnon returned Briseis to Achilles, but the latter had only a short time to enjoy his slave. Neptune was angry with Achilles for killing Cycnus. So he asked Apollo to shoot a discreet arrow and kill him. Apollo did one better. He located Paris, who had pretty much kept himself safe during the war by only tackling poorly-trained, low status Greeks.

Apollo found Paris on the battlefield and reproached him for not trying to kill someone more worthwhile. Then the god pointed Paris' bow and arrow at Achilles' foot, the foot that did not have a protective coating of Styx water. The arrow flew. Guided by Apollo, it found its mark, presumably the great saphenous vein that transports blood to several parts of a hero's body, including his heel. The legendary Achilles bled out and died at the hands of a wife-stealing coward.

Aeneas, who became the father of Rome, also played a heroic part in the battlefield where he killed twenty-eight Greeks. Though he had been raised by Anchises, Aeneas was the son of Venus. She had not been able to resist Anchises' extreme beauty, even though he was a mortal. When Aeneas was born, Venus extracted an oath from Anchises that he would never tell anyone who the mother was. But Anchises found it impossible to keep that promise. Everyone knew.

The gods were very busy during the Trojan war, saving their favourites from imminent death and acting on their petty grudges, while occasionally doing something righteous like getting Hector's body back to old Priam. Venus, in particular, was vigilant about protecting her team. When Diomedes was about to kill Aeneas, Venus saved her son. She also saved Paris when Menelaus was just about to finish him. But when Aeneas went up against Achilles, he had to save himself by fleeing the encounter.

The walls of Troy had been built by Apollo and Neptune; as such, they were unbreakable. Trojan fighters exited the city in an attempt to conquer the Greeks or at least get them running home. But this war was fought outside the walls of Troy for nine years. Trojan wives, aged parents, and children stayed safely inside.

If you were a Trojan wife, your husband might be away at war, but your children and your parents would be safe and fed. This war would rage for years, during which your baby would grow up and learn to read, perhaps. Dinner and breakfast continued to take place at regular intervals.

Then, mysteriously, and for no reason you could think of, the Greeks disappeared. Their camp was gone. Their ships were gone. The fighting was over. The Trojans opened the gates and civilians passed in and out of them, touring the battlefield and rejoicing in their good fortune. The Greeks were gone!

The biggest mystery of all was the giant horse, seemingly made of wood, which the enemy had left behind. The Trojans discussed its many possible meanings. Laocoon, a respected citizen and father living up in the heights of the city, came running down into the town centre, shouting, more or less, 'Are you crazy? Beware of Greeks bearing gifts!'

Okay, that's not exactly what he said, but close. Shadi Bartsch's majestic translation reads, more precisely, 'I fear Greeks, even bringing offerings'. To illustrate his point, Laocoon launched a spear at the wooden beast, but the monolith only issued a groan as if it were hollow.[3] Many of the Trojans knew better, just as the reader probably knows. Truisms like, 'If it sounds too good to be true, it probably is' were bandied about by future Romans.

The Greeks were hiding off the island of Tenemos, a nearby ruin which had been a thriving Trojan suburb before this war. Minerva had helped them build the horse. Virgil describes its construction as pine and 'ribs'.[4] Presumably, these ribs were Minerva's contribution. So let your imagination run wild. I like to think of the horse as pine and titanium.

It might seem that the Greeks had left too much to chance. But there was another phase to their plan. A dishevelled, frightened old man wandered into the city of Troy through the open gates. When questioned, he admitted that he had been part of the Greek army. The crowd of happy, relieved Trojans felt pity for the poor old man, and they begged him to tell his story.

'Where have the Greeks gone?' they wanted to know. He solved that mystery for them. The Greeks had wearied of the war and wished to go home, he lied. But the weather never gave them a good time to set off. They asked Apollo's oracle why they had no victory in the war, and the priest told them that their journey began with a blood sacrifice, so the return trip would require a human sacrifice also.

Nobody volunteered. Their homegrown seer, Calchas, finally named Sinon, the old man who was telling this story, as the human sacrifice. Sinon was sure he had been selected to die because he criticised Greek management of the war. He did not want to die. He escaped and hid overnight in a swamp. Now he was throwing himself on the mercy of the Trojans.

In reality, Sinon was a Greek spy, planted to tell a story that would reconcile the Trojans to this weird horse. He put Ulysses in his story quite often, depicting him as a dishonest schemer, knowing that the Trojans hated him. It may have thrown them off old scent.

Now the Greeks had left, and he would never see his homeland again, Sinon continued. He invited the Trojans to kill him. King Priam was, by this time, part of Sinon's audience, and he personally removed the chains from the storyteller's feet and wrists. Priam assured the old man that he would have a home here in Troy. 'But please tell us, why the horse?' was all Priam asked of this new family member.

Sinon continued his story. Minerva had sided with the Greeks in the war, but she was mad at them now. Ulysses had defiled one of her temples, killing the priests, and stealing her statue, according to Sinon's narrative.

When he got the statue back to camp, it shot fire from its eyes, the goddess was so angry. Calchas, their prophet, said they would never win the war in this round. They must return home, replenish their weapons, placate the gods, and wait for favourable signs. Calchas also told the Greeks to build this huge horse, too big for the Trojans to get inside their gates, Sinon mentioned in passing.

But the Greeks would be back, Sinon insisted, perhaps in a few months, when the gods had guaranteed success. As to the horse, it was a tribute to Minerva, so if the Trojans harmed it, they would anger the goddess. But if they took the horse to the citadel, they would have the victory in the war that was definitely not over.

Around this time, two giant snakes swam toward Troy. They carried their chests and heads above the water, so Trojans could see them approaching. They went straight to Laocoon, who had his two small sons with him. The snakes attacked the children first, biting and mauling, then they looped around Laocoon and throttled him. All three died.

The witnesses took this as a sign that Laocoon was wrong about the horse, and that he had offended the gods by striking 'sacred wood' with his spear.[5] In point of fact, the gods had determined that Troy would fall, and nothing could really save it. Minerva sent the snakes.

Cassandra, a beautiful Trojan princess with the gift of clairvoyance, could see the future fall of Troy, and she desperately tried to warn them. You might remember Cassandra as the daughter of Priam and Hecuba. It was she who identified Paris as their son and Cassandra's brother.

At one time, people had believed Cassandra. But her beauty attracted the god Apollo. He wished to make love to her, but she refused. As we know, the gods could be cruel and arbitrary. Apollo doomed Cassandra to prophesy only the truth while never being believed. So when she tried to warn her family about the horse and the destruction of Troy, they didn't believe her.

It turned out to be relatively easy to get the wooden horse inside Troy's walls. Almost as if it were built for that purpose. The Trojans could actually hear the clank of weapons inside the horse as they dragged it through the city with ropes and wheels. But, by this time, a sort of divine madness had possessed the citizens. They acted as a mob. They got the horse to the citadel, hoping for the gods' favour.

Then the Trojans went to bed, and Sinon unlatched the horse's storage compartment while the Greek fleet sailed stealthily back from Tenedos to the shores of Troy. Ulysses lowered himself out of the horse on a rope along with Menelaus, the wronged husband; Neoptolemus, Achilles' son; Epeus, the horse's builder, and several other warriors. They opened the city gates to the rest of the fighters. Then: chaos, madness, destruction.

Just before screams and flames filled the streets, dead Hector appeared to Aeneas in a dream. Hector's beard was drenched in blood, and he bore all the wounds and scars he had earned in battle. After killing him, Achilles had dragged Troy's hero behind his chariot, until he was black and swollen with blood and dirt. This was the ghost that came to Aeneas.

'Get out', Hector said.

He went on to explain, quickly, that Troy was finished. Aeneas was his people's hope now. He was to gather some religious icons, rally his family along with any survivors, and set sail for other lands.

Aeneas lived with his father, Anchises. Their house was just out of the city centre, buffered by trees, so it took a few minutes for the anguished shouts of surprise and defeat to reach Aeneas' ears. He climbed up on his father's roof and saw a palace fall to fire. The neighbouring dwelling fell next.

A passion for fighting seized him. He grabbed a sword. To die in battle seemed, suddenly, glorious. But that was not to be his fate. Hector had already told him what he must do.

Panthus came running to Aeneas' door. He was a priest of Apollo. When Aeneas asked him to point out the heart of battle, Panthus insisted that Troy was done.

'Cruel Jupiter has given everything to Argos', he said.[6] The horse they had so proudly dragged to the citadel was vomiting fighters. Sinon, the old man they had so pitied, was feeding Trojans to a bonfire.

Aeneas met up with some friends, and they were all spoiling to fight to the death. One of them, Coroebus, was engaged to King Priam's daughter, Cassandra. They met a band of Greek plunderers who mistook Aeneas and his friends for fellow Greeks.

The real Greeks were far too slow in recognising their mistake. Aeneas and company slaughtered them and put on their armour so that they could pass as Greeks and commit more atrocities. They rampaged through the city, killing as the night provided opportunity.

They saw Cassandra being dragged by the hair from a temple, her wrists in ropes. Coroebus, her betrothed, seethed with uncontrolled anger and got himself killed trying to defend her. The Greek fighters finally heard the Trojans' accents and knew they were in disguise. In the ensuing fight, many of Aeneas' comrades were killed.

The Greeks then attacked King Priam's palace. Priam's unarmed family and servants desperately threw objects out the windows in an attempt to deter the fighters and save themselves. A band of Trojans shot arrows from the roof. Mostly, these arrows just fell on Greek shields.

The Greeks had ladders. They scaled Priam's home. When the roof fighters saw their enemy's progress, they started throwing pieces of the roof and battlements. Aeneas and his two remaining fighters used a tunnel behind the palace to reach the roof. They joined several others in detaching a tower and throwing it on the ground, where it crushed a number of Greeks.

Neoptolemus took a double axe to the front palace door and finally breached the interior. Soon the guard was killed, and soldiers crowded into Priam's spacious house. What the Greeks found inside was mostly just women crying and kissing door posts, knowing that they were about to be enslaved.

Priam had fifty sons, nineteen of them with his lawfully wedded Hecuba. Their palace must have been quite spacious because Hecuba had made space for fifty wedded couples and all their children. The marauding Greeks found Priam and Hecuba at their family altar along with their daughters in law.

Shaking, Priam had put on his armour, but Hecuba convinced him to take sanctuary at the altar with her. They should have been safe there.

One of Priam's sons, Polites, came running in, pursued by Neoptolemus, who killed him with a spear right in front of his mother and father.

Priam raged at Neoptolemus, accusing him of dishonour and of lying about being Achilles' son. Achilles had, at the very least, given Priam Hector's body to bury properly. And here is Neoptolemus, killing a boy right in his father's sight line.

The old man feebly threw his spear at Neoptolemus. The tip lodged ineffectively in the centre of the Greek's bronze shield and hung there. As he was killing Priam, Neoptolemus quipped that the old king would meet Achilles in hell. Priam could tell Achilles all about the bad deeds of his son, the Greek added.

Aeneas found Priam gasping out the last seconds of his life. While observing the old king, Aeneas remembered that he, himself, had a father. And a wife. His rage gave way to reflection. The companions with whom he had dived into battle were all dead.

He wandered the streets of burning Troy alone. Then he saw Helen, hiding out in the temple of Vesta, the very private goddess of domesticity. Rage re-entered his heart. He thought of her going safely home and enjoying the company of Trojan captives, boys and girls that would be taken now as slaves. Why should she live when her betters had died in battle? As he prepared to kill Helen, Venus appeared to him.

Was this the same Venus who had bribed Paris for that golden apple? It was, and yet it was not. This Venus, the mother of Aeneas, had loved a mere mortal. The love of the gods for mortals is generally a momentary thing. But this Venus, Virgil's Venus, held her former lover in her heart. And she loved her mortal son. In her son's life, she was frequently a peacemaker. She was very different from Apuleius' petty and entitled Venus.

She urged Aeneas to turn his attention to his family. Helen was not to blame for the fall of Troy, Venus insisted. It was a collaborative effort of the gods. Even now, Neptune was shaking the city walls. Minerva was watching from a height. Juno had strapped on a sword and was directing troops. Even Jupiter wanted this – this destruction. With words like these, the love goddess convinced Aeneas that he could do nothing to save Troy. Instead, he must save Anchises, his wife Creusa, and his son Ascanius.

When he finally returned to his home, he found that Anchises would not leave. He would find a Greek to kill him, the old man declared. He did not wish to survive the fall of Troy. Helpless, Aeneas did what seemed right. He put his armour back on and prepared to re-enter the battle. But at the door, his wife, Creusa, crumpled at his feet and begged him to protect her and their family.

Or else she would prefer to go and die with him. She begged him to think of his son, and then the family received two omens. A harmless fire shot out of Ascanius' head. Was it a sign? Of course it was! Anchises prayed to Jupiter. If the gods were pleased with the family's piety, confirm the sign, he asked. Immediately, Jupiter answered with the crash of thunder, and a shooting star arced across the sky, visible above Troy's remaining rooftops.

Venus' old lover finally got the message. The gods were telling them to go. The old man got to his feet, but he was very frail. Aeneas lifted his father onto his back, where Anchises held on to his son's neck. Aeneas took his small son by the hand and told his wife to follow them.

He instructed the servants to break up and take different routes. They would all meet at a cypress tree near the abandoned shrine to Ceres. Anchises had to carry the household gods. Aeneas dared not touch them until he was purified of his recent killings. Purification required running water.

Now, Aeneas was leading his family through the burning streets of Troy. Before, he had been so casual with his life, but, holding his son's hand, feeling his father's hands on his neck, now he was afraid. They heard the clang of weapons coming near them, Anchises said, 'run', and Aeneas panicked.

He ran, but when they came to the cypress tree, he saw that they had lost Creusa. Desperate, he retraced his steps, braved the walls again, and recklessly called her name as he searched. It occurred to him that she might have gone back to the house. He found it in flames. He stopped by Priam's palace and saw Ulysses guarding Trojan treasure – family altars, golden bowls, heaps of clothing, as well as the human cargo – wives and children who would be trafficked when the Greeks had cast lots for them.

His quest came to an end when his wife's ghost appeared to him. He had expected to find her alive, and the sight of her dead shade terrified him. But her purpose was only to comfort him, and remind him of all he had yet to save.

She did not say how she had died. She was grateful not to become a Greek slave, she said, but she was not destined to leave Troy. As a shade, she could see the future. Aeneas would travel to Hesperia, and he would receive a kingdom to rule, with a royal bride.

'Love our son', she commanded and then disappeared.[7]

Around this time, the Greeks were deciding what to do about Astyanax. He was just a small boy, the son of Hector and Andromache. He was no immediate threat to the Greeks who had already plundered Troy.

But he was a grandson to King Priam. It would be his life's mission to avenge his family and city, the Greeks assumed. So they pushed the boy off a high tower and killed him in cold blood.

When Aeneas arrived at the rendezvous point, he found that many Trojans had already joined his rescue mission. All of Troy was in flames. They had no homes, no possessions except what little they could carry. They looked to Aeneas for leadership.

They were 'prepared to cross the sea to any land I chose', Aeneas observed with humility and genuine awe.[8] Talk about an accidental hero. He had been elected, by default and mere survival, to lead his people to a new homeland.

And so he would.

Chapter 9

Aftermath

It was Ajax who dragged the royal priestess Cassandra out of Apollo's temple. His ships and those of Agamemnon, Ulysses, and Menelaus left Troy at the same time. But the gods who formerly favoured them were angered by the desecration of Cassandra and the murder of Astyanax. They whipped up a storm that wrecked many Greek ships on the Capharean rocks. Minerva threw the lightning bolt that killed Ajax, who was also dashed on the rocks for good measure.

Palamedes' murder had not been forgotten, at least not by his father, Nauplius. Nauplius had also fought with the Greeks, but he nursed a grudge. When the storm landed them on the rocks, he saw an opportunity to get even. Somehow he made it to shore where he raised a large torch. The Greeks who had not yet broken their ships on the rocks saw the torch. They thought that Nauplius was guiding them to safety.

He was not. He guided them to their deaths. Many ships were lured to the rocks, and many men spilled their guts and died there. If they managed to survive and climb out, alive, from the rocks, Nauplius was there to finish them off. His revenge would never be perfect, however. Palamedes' true murderer was Ulysses who would, against all odds, return to Ithaca alive.

That storm broke up the combined fleet, and Menelaus' ships and men were blown all the way to Egypt. There, Menelaus consulted the legendary Proteus, a seer, sailor, and shape shifter. This Proteus gave Menelaus the bad news. Even though the gods had definitely helped the Greeks win the war, they were now angry at the fall of Troy. This anger could not be placated with an ordinary sacrifice. Menelaus must perform a hecatomb, which is the sacrifice of a thousand heads of cattle.

Menelaus performed the hecatomb and was allowed to return to Sparta, eight years after winning Troy.[1]

Agamemnon

Agamemnon returned home with more than just his naked self, but his homecoming was not a joyous occasion, either. After his war victories, he lost the majority of his ships in a terrible storm, with a fog so thick, the ships were crashing into each other. Many sank, and many returned to Argos with substantial damage.

For Clytemnestra, ten years was not long enough for her husband to be gone. By the time Agamemnon returned, she had entered into a serious affair with Aegisthus, who had pretensions to Agamemnon's throne. The two of them had effectively been ruling Argos in the king's long absence.

Clytemnestra had not forgotten Iphigenia's death, which she considered a murder. And now Agamemnon had arrived home with yet another mistress. He was 'mad with passion for a sacred maid',[2] she complained. Cassandra, Troy's high priestess, she of the precise predictions, was now Agamemnon's sex slave. Chriseis, another of Agamemnon's sex slaves, had been the daughter of a priest. It does seem that he had a type.

But it was customary for a war victor to come home with riches and slaves, and Agamemnon had done nothing especially dishonourable, by his own standards. From his point of view, he was enriching his kingdom. From Clytemnestra's point of view, he was an unfaithful, absentee husband, a child killer, and a defiler of priestesses.

In Seneca, the Younger's, *Agamemnon*, Clytemnestra debates whether she should kill her husband or not. She is mindful that cultural norms give Agamemnon broad sway. Then she remembers Helen, her sister, who has ruined all of Europe and Asia, Clytemnestra exaggerates. Helen and Menelaus have reconciled, at Agamemnon's behest, and they have resumed their life in Sparta. If *those two* can reconcile, anybody can, she muses.

At this point in her reverie, Aegisthus interrupts with this intrusive thought: 'Yes, but Menelaus never gave his heart to a mistress'. Aegisthus also speculates that war has hardened Agamemnon. He left Mycenae a king; he will return a tyrant, he predicts.[3]

First Clytemnestra gives her husband a hand-made garment to put on. This garment turns out to be impossible to take off as Aegisthus is striking Agamemnon with a knife. Aegisthus takes too long. In a rage, Clytemnestra attacks her husband with an axe and severs his head from his body. When Electra, her daughter by Agamemnon, confronts Clytemnestra for her father's murder, Clytemnestra again recites the list of her grievances. Before she can be taken captive, Electra secures a foster home for her baby brother, Orestes, to save him from Astyanax's fate.

As the curtain falls, Electra is being dragged off stage to exile. Cassandra is about to be executed under orders from Clytemnestra. That Trojan princess, doomed to foretell the truth without being believed, has the last word. The Greeks, she says, have now suffered losses equivalent to those of Troy. She is happy to have lived this long, having seen Agamemnon slain, and Argive ships lost. Her last words are to Clytemnestra, predicting her murder at the hands of Electra and her son, Orestes.

But, of course, Clytemnestra won't heed her warning.

Ulysses

Ulysses was not the first man to leave his wife for twenty years, but he might be the most famous of those who did. It took ten years to defeat the Trojans. The return home took him another ten years.

If you look at a map that shows the locations of ancient Troy, now part of Turkey, and Ithaca, Ulysses' home, you will immediately see that a land route would have been faster and safer. In the process of directing his ships across a few miles of the Aegean, he would lose his entire fleet and his entire crew. He would end up literally drifting in the ocean, a man without a boat, until he washed up on a random shore where a pretty girl took pity on him.

If Ulysses' wife, Penelope, had seen a modern map, she might have asked different questions, like 'Did you think to just take a horse?' I haven't tested this theory, but I'm pretty sure you could charter a fishing boat to travel from Troy to Ithaca today. In recent news, desperate people have been mad enough to swim across the Aegean from Turkey to Greece.

My point is that the journeys of the ancients often seem like they must encompass a geographical area roughly the size of Europe, Asia, and Australia. But, in fact, they encompassed the area you would call Greece, Italy, Turkey, and North Africa. And yet, the distance could seem mythic when transportation was in its infancy, and especially when anything went wrong.

Things frequently went wrong for Ulysses, better known to some readers by his Greek name, Odysseus. If you need to know exactly how wrong, you will need to read the Greek poets, mainly Homer. The Greek Odysseus is a tragic figure let down by pretty much everyone in his life, except immediate family. His men have no appropriate sense of caution or piety. They commit pointless blasphemy, petty theft, and get themselves killed. His neighbours back in Ithaca are no better. They pronounce him dead and then proceed to rob his estate of everything it is worth.

Ulysses, as the Romans styled him, was kind of a crook. You might call him an early antihero. In the Roman view, the gift horse was a dishonourable ruse, something that would definitely have been questioned under the Geneva Convention. But even Ovid, who stood for the ancient Roman sense of order and civility, had to admire Ulysses' cleverness and storytelling ability.

After ransacking Troy, Ulysses and his men found themselves on the island of the cyclopes, a race of giant cannibals, each with one eye. Polyphemus was one of their number. He was the son of Neptune and the sea goddess, Thoosa.

Polyphemus was immortal, but not invulnerable, as Ulysses would prove. The one-eyed giant was kind of a genetic throwback to the titans who often spawned monsters. Even though he lived very remotely, Polyphemus had heard Ulysses' name. Specifically, he had heard a prophecy that a man named Ulysses would rob him of his sight. Somehow, Ulysses intuited that he should not tell this monster who he really was. So he introduced himself as Utis (also spelled Outis).[4]

When Ulysses and his men landed on the cyclops' shores, Polyphemus took them captive, confining them to the cave where he kept his sheep at night. It was a vast habitat, but dark and nasty with splattered blood and body parts. He blocked this cave with a giant rock which he personally rolled back when he wished to enter or leave.

For a cannibal and murderer, Polyphemus was surprisingly tender with his sheep. He grazed them every day, keeping a watchful eye on them. At the end of the day, they would return to the safety of the cyclops' cave.

This gentle care was not applied to the Ithacan prisoners. When he had selected two men out of Ulysses' crew to dine on, he dashed their brains against the cave floor and then ate them raw. He always ate men two at a time. It was a good time to panic, but Ulysses kept his nerve. He offered Polyphemus some wine that Ulysses had been gifted.

When Polyphemus fell asleep, drunk and sated on Ulysses' crew, he burped up a mixture of wine, mixed with Ithacan blood. Ulysses and his men surrounded him and plunged their spears into his one eye. Roaring in pain at the loss of his eyesight, the cyclops awoke and raged. He pushed back the boulder of his cave.

Ulysses was ready for that. To get them out of the cave, he had tethered his men to the underbellies of Polyphemus' sheep. When Polyphemus exited, the sheep walked out with the hidden Ithacans. Ulysses had placed himself under the largest ram he could find out of the flock and hung on to the animal's fur for dear life as it left the cave.

Polyphemus used a pine tree trunk as a crutch and blindly made his way down to the sea, where he washed off the blood oozing from his eye socket. He summoned the other cyclops, who came out of their respective caves to see what all the racket was about.

But when he told them that 'Utis' had blinded him, he may have finally realized that Utis means 'no one' in Greek. So he was screaming out that no one had blinded him.

Freed from the cave, the Ithacan crew ran to their ships, and Ulysses yelled insults at Polyphemus, making him even angrier. The Ithacan hero had carefully withheld his real name, but as the ships were leaving, he could not stop himself from bragging that he was the King of Ithaca and that he had gotten the better of a cyclops.

Enraged, Polyphemus tore off a part of a nearby mountain and threw it into the sea, but the expert rowing of the Greeks saved their ships. They did not realise until it was too late that they had left behind their comrade, Achaemenides. He survived on berries, grass, leaves, and acorns for three months, in hiding, haunted by the memory of

Polyphemus grabbing his colleagues, two at a time, and dashing their brains against the ground, before squatting to eat them raw.

He remembered the blood in the giant's beard and how he spewed gobbets of food and wine as he cannibalised the Greeks. As if the fear of a violent death were not enough, Achaemenides also feared dying without any rites. In the stomach of a monster, his shade – the consciousness that survived death – would have no peace. It would not be able to cross the Styx or see the Elysian Fields.

After many days of hiding in terror, Achaemenides saw a ship. He made his way to shore and signalled. The ship picked him up. It was the Trojans in exile. Achaemenides' journey will be picked up later in this book.

Having escaped Polyphemus, Ulysses sought the help of the deity Aeolus, keeper of the winds. Aeolus graciously gave the Greek hero an ox-skin bag of all the winds. By releasing wind from the bag judiciously, Ulysses was able to keep all his ships afloat and safe for nine straight days, and the rugged island of Ithaca was in their sight. They were home.

But not quite. His crew did not understand the purpose of the wind bag. They thought it contained treasure that Ulysses was not sharing with them. Their homeland was only hours or minutes away, so they mutinied and opened the sack. The uncontained winds blew them all the way back across the Aegean to the home of Aeolus, from whom they had departed only nine days ago. Correctly perceiving that this voyage was cursed, Aeolus retracted his earlier hospitality and told the Ithacans to get lost.

They next landed on an island of cannibals. The king promptly devoured one of three messengers that Ulysses sent to parlay with him. When they learned the violent nature of the island, the Ithacans swiftly got in their ships and prepared to disembark. But the islanders surged onto the beach and threw rocks and tree branches at the fleet, sinking all but the one ship on which Ulysses sailed.

The remaining crew washed up on the island of Circe. Remembering the hostile greeting they had received from Polyphemus, many of Ulysses' men thought they should avoid interactions with the natives. But they needed food and water, wood for repairs, tools, and protective clothing. They ended up drawing lots to see who would visit the palace and ask for help.

When they reached the threshold, they were rushed by wolves, bears, and lions. These beasts acted strangely, however. Instead of attacking the men, they approached in a friendly manner, wagging their tails and licking the hands of the Ithacan guests. Servants admitted the Ithacans to the palace and there they saw Circe, a powerful goddess attended by nymphs and nereids. Circe's ladies in waiting were busily weaving grasses and arranging flowers while Circe sat on her throne in a beautiful dress wrapped in a gold cloak.

Circe greeted the men graciously, and she offered them hospitality, as the gods strongly recommend. Her servants prepared a dish consisting of barley, honey, wine, and curdled milk to which Circe added some 'juices'. When they had devoured this potion, Circe tapped them each on the head with her wand, and they all turned into pigs. Only Eurylochus had declined to dine, so he was the one who returned to Ulysses to report that twenty-one of his men had been shape shifted without consent.

When he heard Eurylochus' report, Ulysses proceeded to Circe's palace. Mercury flew down to him on the wings that graced his sandals and helmet. He gave Ulysses an antidote to Circe's transforming potion.

Ulysses drank the antidote. When Circe tapped him on the head, expecting him to turn into a pig, he drew his sword on her. His ruthlessness surprised Circe and, it appears, also aroused her. The two of them struck a deal. He would become her lover if she would restore his crew to their humanity and pose no further harm to any of them.

Even though she was a minor goddess, mythologists often refer to Circe as a witch, and it raises the question: What is the difference between a witch and a goddess? They can both do magic.

It seems to be a matter of scholarship. Goddesses are born with power. Witches, however, have to study. Circe prays to unknown gods and uses a language the poets do not recognise. So it must be the language of sorcery.

This added layer of arcane knowledge distinguishes the witch from the nymph or naiad, whose magic is innate, not learned. That's why witches, like Medea, can start out as ordinary human girls, then develop a talent for dark magic through study and devotion to the more sinister deities.

Ulysses and his men lived on Circe's island for a year, while she shared hospitality. Ulysses had two children with her. Their names were Nausithous and Telegonus, according to Hyginus.[5]

Eventually, after that very long rest, they longed for their homes again. But Circe warned Ulysses that he must first sojourn to the land of the dead and ask for advice from the prophet Tiresias. Ulysses had, unintentionally, offended Neptune by blinding the god's son, Polyphemus. Only Tiresias could tell Ulysses how to placate Neptune and return home.

He approached the underworld from Lake Avernus, an Italian crater lake. In Hyginus' stripped down version of Ulysses' adventures, he gets a message from Tiresias that he should respect the cattle of the sun god, if he hopes to see home again.[6] He also meets Elpenor, one of his recent crew members who had made it all the way to Circe's island and then disappeared.

Elpenor had gotten drunk and fallen off a ladder, as he now explained to Ulysses. His mortal remains were without a proper burial, and his spirit could not make peace with that. He begged Ulysses to backtrack to Circe and bury his bones. Ulysses also saw his mother, Anticlia, and they talked of his journey.

He then returned to Circe long enough to bury his crew member. Elpenor had requested that a boat rudder be placed on his grave, and Ulysses complied. After all, it was a dead man's request and a small thing to let him be remembered as a sailor and not as someone who couldn't mix wine with climbing.

Ulysses' ability to see and hear the sirens without falling victim to them is legendary. They were the daughters of Achelous, a river god, and one of the muses. They were women from the waist up and chickens from the waist down. They sound very silly, indeed, but they were lethal. No man could hear them singing without wanting to be near them.

They were surrounded by wreckage. Ship parts were scattered on nearby rocks. Whole ship crews had drowned or had their bodies broken. The sirens are the perfect metaphor for dangerous knowledge. They have the most beautiful singing voices, but no one can hear them and live.

The immortality of the sirens was linked to this paradox. A prophecy said they would become vulnerable to death only after someone had heard their songs and lived. That unique mortal was fated to be Ulysses.

Fortunately, Circe had warned Ulysses of these creatures. He told his men that, after they had tied him to the mast, they must put wax in their ears. With this strategy, the clever Ithacan got past the sirens and broke their spell. He had heard their song and lived. Now they could die.

Several of Ulysses' adventures would be repeated by Aeneas and the Trojans in exile. The Scylla and Charybdis problem was one of these. There was no avoiding it. Ulysses would have to steer his one remaining ship between a deadly whirlpool, named Charybdis, and a monster with six cannibal heads, named Scylla. His decision to sacrifice six of his men, who would be randomly selected by Scylla, was textbook utilitarian thinking. Machiavelli had nothing on Ulysses.

They landed their last remaining ship on the island where the sun god grazed his golden cattle. It should have been obvious to anyone that these beasts were not ordinary. They glowed.

Ulysses had been warned about the ownership of these bulls, so he told his men, under no circumstances, to touch the cattle. But those men hadn't eaten well since leaving Circe. As we all know, piety is easily swamped by needs more fundamental on Maslow's hierarchy. As soon as their leader went to sleep, his men killed several bulls and roasted them. The meat hollered while it was being cooked, and they probably knew there was no walking this back. They had made a new immortal enemy.

The violation was so unthinkable that Jupiter became involved. As soon as the men were back at sea, he destroyed their ship with a lightning bolt. All the men were killed save one – Ulysses, who washed up, barely alive, on the island of Ogygia. This turned out to be Calypso's island. She was a nymph and daughter of Atlas.

What was it about Ulysses that so enchanted women? By this point in his life, he had to be at least 40. He had been blown around on the Aegean for years without sunscreen or smart fabrics, much less a tailor or dermatologist. No source gives us any reason to believe that Ulysses' appeal was in his looks.

But he was a talented storyteller. Whatever the attraction, Calypso, like Circe, fell for it and held Ulysses in a soft hostage situation for a year as her lover. Finally, Jupiter relented. Though he had destroyed Ulysses' skeleton crew and remaining ship, he now sent Mercury with a message. The winged god flew to Calypso and told her that she must release Ulysses so that he could complete his journey.

The goddess was generous with Ulysses, even though he was leaving against her will. She gave him a raft and supplies. But she was not powerful enough to guard him against Neptune's ongoing wrath. The god of tidal waves and hurricanes was still nursing his anger at the blinding of

Polyphemus. Once Ulysses was out of Calypso's sight, Neptune dashed the hero's raft to pieces and left him thrashing, rudderless, in the waves.

An ancient sea goddess, Leucothoe, felt sorry for the Ithacan, so she tethered him to her and prevented him from drowning. He made his way to another island where he collapsed, once again, on a foreign beach. It was the island of the Phaeacians. Ulysses had nothing to recommend himself – he had no jewellery, no robe, no luggage. Every bit of clothing had been ripped off him in the ocean.

Modestly, he hid himself in a pile of leaves to hide his nakedness. Nausicaa, the king's daughter, found him there. She had gone down to the water to wash some clothes. Ulysses asked her for help. She gave him a cloak and applied some empathy. Naked Ulysses was a character test for the Phaeacians. Would they treat him with the same courtesy and kindness they would apply to friends and relatives?

Yes, they would. In fact, Nausicaa was already falling in love with him even though, realistically, he was at least twice her age. She escorted him back to her father's palace, where King Alcinous would wine and dine our hero and, of course, ask his story. These hosts were perfectly behaved and, if Nausicaa had feelings for Ulysses, they were honourable, and she did not try to detain him when she heard that he longed to return to his wife and son.

The Phaeacians gave him a ship and loaded it with expensive gifts. But even then, at the end of his journey, Ulysses could not escape the gods' wrath. According to Hyginus, it was Mercury who destroyed the Phaeacian gift ship.[7] All Ulysses' treasure, the gifts of the generous Alcinous and his daughter, was lost.

However, he was within swimming distance of Penelope, so he swam, defeated, weather-beaten, and broke, just as the prophecy had foretold. He had lost all twelve ships, and dozens of crew members and fighters. He was alone, moneyless, naked, sun baked beyond recognition.

And, in fact, no one recognized him, except for the nurse who raised him as a child. What he came home to was basically a home invasion. Many, if not all, of the young men of Ithaca had infested Ulysses' estate.

They were in the wine cellar, choosing which wines to pair with today's feast. They were in the stables, deciding which head of livestock to slaughter. They were in the bedrooms having sex with Ulysses' servants.

Officially, they were there to woo Penelope. They had all declared their intention to marry her. She was, in fact, very beautiful. But the suitors mostly wanted her estate now that Ulysses was surely dead, or so they believed.

These 'suitors' had given themselves the run of Penelope's house and grounds. There was no open talk of raping Ulysses' widow, only because the home invaders believed that her husband would be the next king of Ithaca. The belief that she would eventually choose a second husband offered Penelope a thin layer of protection, but not so much safety that she could actually throw the thugs out of her house.

Ithaca had a reputation as a barbarian nation. Now its young men were living up to that. Waiting for Ulysses to come home, delaying the suitors, keeping her grown son Telemachus safe – it was a careful balancing act for Penelope.

She was running a long con on the suitors. She'd promised that she would marry when she had finished weaving a shroud for her father in law. By day, within sight of the suitors, she virtuously worked her fabric. Under cover of night, she tore up the day's work. She never made any real progress on the shroud. The suitors didn't notice? Apparently, there is truth to the proverb that a woman's work is never done, *and* men have no idea what we do all day.

Ulysses immediately understood that these suitors were potential murderers and that he would do well not to confront them without doing more reconnaissance.

Also, *and this is important*, he had no weapons.

After twenty years, it was understandable if few people recognised him. But, just to make sure, Minerva changed his appearance, making him look even more ragged and beaten than he was. His dog recognised him, though. Minerva would have to change his smell to fool the dog.

As he was stealthily approaching his own homestead, in disguise, Ulysses found his swineherd, Eumaeus. This loyal employee told our hero the whole story of Penelope's home arrest. Soon the suitors affirmed it by showing up to steal some more pigs.

Eumaeus invited Ulysses to share his humble hut, for which the Ithacan king was grateful. Minerva restored Ulysses to his original appearance, and the swineherd finally recognised him, hugging him and crying for joy. They agreed that the swineherd would lead his king to the palace on the following morning.

Again, Minerva transformed Ulysses' appearance so that he looked like a beggar when he entered his own home and saw the suitors. Eumaeus introduced Ulysses to the invaders, explaining that they would now have a second beggar to amuse them. One of the suitors proposed a fight. In the ensuing contest, Ulysses body slammed Irus, a real beggar, who ran away at the first opportunity.

Next, Eumaeus introduced the new 'beggar' to Euryclia, Ulysses' childhood nurse. She recognised him instantly, despite the god-given disguise. He clamped his hand over her mouth to keep her from revealing his identity.

He still didn't have any weapons.

In a whisper, presumably, he told Euryclia to bring out his bow and arrows and announce a contest. Whosoever could string Ulysses' bow would get to marry Penelope and take over what was left of Ulysses' estate. Euryclia obeyed, but none of the suitors could string that bow. Ulysses strung his bows really, really tight.

The thing about a really tightly strung bow is that, if you *can* pull back the string, it shoots the arrow with a great deal of force and speed. But how to get the bow into the hands of its true owner? Eumaeus' timing was perfect.

After the suitors had tired of giving it a go, he joked, 'Hey, maybe the beggar should have a try!' Despite some grumbling, the bow and arrows were handed to Ulysses. At last.

Hyginus doesn't waste a lot of words on this scene. The seeming beggar could and did string the bow of the great Ulysses. The mistake the home invaders had made was to give him weapons. He killed them all in short order.

Hyginus' Ulysses has a short peaceful family reunion of uncertain duration. Then Circe sent her son by Ulysses to visit his father. His name was Telegonus. A storm raged, and Telegonus was tossed up on the shores of Ithaca, alone and starving.

He foraged off the land until Ulysses and Telemachus found and confronted him, not knowing who he was. In the ensuing fight, Telegonus killed Ulysses. Minerva descended and commanded the survivors –

Telegonus, Telemachus, and Penelope – to travel to Circe's island and give Ulysses' body to that goddess, so that she could lay him to rest.

The family did as the goddess required. Then Penelope married Telegonus, and the two of them had a son named Italus. He gave his name to the country of Italy. Telemachus married Circe, and their son, Latinus, gave his name to the Latin language. So, in the very, very end, even Ulysses became a tool of the Roman empire, providing descendants whose very names would ring with its greatness.

It's a stark ending for so divisive a hero. The ancients felt no compulsion to provide a happy ending to a story of terrible struggle in the way even our most ruthless contemporary filmmakers feel they must. But it was not the only ending a poet could imagine for Ulysses.

Tennyson imagined the Ithacan getting bored of domestic life. He enjoys a few years with his wife, ruling his kingdom, but then he hands the keys of government to Telemachus, gathers a few men, and takes off again. He does not propose ever to return home:

> for my purpose holds
> To sail beyond the sunset, and the baths
> Of all the western stars, until I die.

Tennyson's Ulysses declares that either they will drown, or they will arrive at the 'Happy Isles' where Tennyson's Achilles now lives in a joyous afterlife. Our hero acknowledges that he is old and lacks the strength of his youth. Still, he will not squander his old age in simple domestic pleasures when there is still a world largely unexplored out there:

> Tho' much is taken, much abides; and tho'
> We are not now that strength which in old days
> Moved earth and heaven, that which we are, we are;
> One equal temper of heroic hearts,
> Made weak by time and fate, but strong in will
> To strive, to seek, to find, and not to yield.[8]

Chapter 10

The Fall of Troy; the Rise of Rome

While the Greeks were drawing lots and dividing up the spoils of Troy, the Trojan survivor, Aeneas, was leading his remaining people to build a fleet out of their pine trees. By summer, they were ready to sail. Aeneas wept to leave the familiar shores of his homeland. When they landed on a friendly island, he went to the shrine of Apollo and prayed for guidance:

> Apollo, give my weary people walls, a home,
> a lineage and lasting city. Save this second
> Troy, the ruins left by cruel Achilles and
> the Greeks. Who will lead us? Where to settle?[1]

Early in their journey, the Trojans landed on the island of Crete, and Virgil does not tell his readers how long they were there. But they had time for several weddings, growing some crops, and building walls and houses. They were so settled that Aeneas asked his people to build a citadel. But then, in just a few metric lines, it all came crashing down.

Crops failed, Trojans fell ill, many died. Gods visited Aeneas in his sleep and told him that he must take the Trojan remnant and depart this land. Crete was not the home they were destined for. When he told his father, Anchises remembered a prophecy of Cassandra's that no one believed at the time – she had frequently spoken of Italy and their future there.

Reassured by Anchises, the Trojans set off to sea again, this time looking west. They were lost for three days in a black out fog. Then they landed on the island of the Strophades. This was the home of the harpies, giant birds with claws, and the faces of starving girls. They were most famous for defecating inappropriately, a gift they weaponised.

The hungry Trojans saw some sheep and cattle when they landed, and they wasted no time slaughtering enough to eat, while quickly lighting pyres for the gods and asking them to partake of the upcoming feast. The harpies descended on their meal, tore up the food and defecated so thoroughly that the site was ruined.

The Trojans moved to a more private space, but the harpies found them there, too. Finally, Aeneas ordered his men to attack the beasts. But the birds could not be harmed. Trojan blades bounced off their backs and feathers. Celeano, their leader, landed on a tree and spoke directly to Aeneas.

'Oh, you will reach Italy, all right', was approximately what she said, 'but not until all of you have been so hungry, you will eat your tables. And that will be your punishment for your attack on us. Apollo promised me'.[2] Aeneas' men were shaken by this prophecy. The Trojans left those shores and eventually reached Chaonia. There Aeneas saw Andromache, Hector's widow and a former princess of Troy. She fainted when she saw Aeneas and then, when she had recovered, told him her story. The Greeks had drawn lots for the Trojan captives. She had been taken prisoner by Neoptolemus, Achilles' son, but he handed her off to Helenus, her fellow Trojan slave and the brother of the late Hector.

Neoptolemus died, and Helenus inherited part of the latter's kingdom. He and Andromache were converted instantly from slaves to king and queen of their own land. They built a 'little Troy', complete with a tower and a small stream that they named after the Xanthus River back in Troy. They celebrated their reunion with other Trojans at a great feast and served food on gold plates and wine in bowls.

The wandering Trojan remnant must have felt some shame and confusion. Here they had been traveling for years without getting a foothold, and Andromache and Helenus had reestablished a mini version of Troy, right here in Greece. The reversal of their bad fortune seemed so easy.

Aeneas confided in Helenus about Celeano's curse. Helenus escorted him to their Apollonian temple. When Aeneas heard the priest call him 'goddess-born', he believed that the words came directly from Apollo.

The news was both good and bad. They would arrive in Italy, Apollo said through this priest, but it would not be easy. They would have to cross the Sicilian sea, the salt waters of Italy, the lake of Avernus, and Circe's island. Evil Greeks had already settled the coast of Italy that was facing Little Troy. They should not seek to settle there. The portent that Aeneas should be looking for is this:

> When a huge sow meets your worried eyes,
> By a lonely stream, with oak-lined banks,
> lying on the ground with thirty in her litter,
> the piglets at her teats all white, herself white too:
> that place will be your city, and an end to hardship.[3]

So that Aeneas would not have to choose between Scylla and Charybdis, as Ulysses had done, the priest channelling Apollo said to go the long way around. They would have to go around Sicily and find a spot on the western shore of Italy, the further shore, not the close one.

Nor could Aeneas avoid the requisite trip to the underworld, the priest explained. There was a semi-mad sybil in a deep cave off Lake Avernus. Aeneas must find her. She would tell him his future; hearing her, he would be forewarned about the perils to come. Finally, the Trojans must pay special attention to Juno in their religious rites, the priest urged.

Apollo's priest in Little Troy understood the importance of the Trojan journey, and he sent gifts of silver and copper directly to their ships. Among the gifts he gave were the weapons and armour of Neoptolemus. The Trojans also received gifts of horses, armaments, and human resources: extra rowers and guides. They readied their ships, and Andromache came out with gifts of gold-embroidered clothing. She fawned over Ascanius, Aeneas' son, who was so similar to her murdered Astyanax.

The ships left Little Troy and sailed until they saw the eastern shores of Italy. Suddenly, they found themselves in boiling shallows with the ocean roaring in their ears. Anchises shouted that they had stumbled upon Charybdis, the mythic whirlpool that those who sailed between Sicily and Italy encountered.

The whirlpool sucked them all the way down to Hades, Virgil writes, yet they survived, returned to the surface of the sea. Released from

Charybdis without harm, they drifted to the island of the Cyclops, the same island on which Ulysses had blinded Polyphemus. The weather was so bad, they had no choice but to land and pass the night.

Achaemenides, Ulysses' abandoned comrade, came running toward them. He begged the Trojans to take him with them or kill him. At least he would die by human hands, he noted. Anchises reached out to this poor soul and promised to protect him.

Their new crew member warned the Trojans not to stay on that island. There were a hundred cyclopes living there, not just the blinded Polyphemus. As they were speaking, Polyphemus appeared on a height above them, and they watched as he lumbered down to shore, using a pine tree as a crutch. His eye wound was still raw and oozing. It had not healed in the three months since Ulysses had escaped with his Ithacan remnant.

The Trojans needed no further warnings. They jumped on their ships and started rowing, along with Achaemenides who had quickly pledged his life to their service. Their rowing churned up the water enough to alert Polyphemus who set up a howl so loud, it shook the water and could be heard far inland. His howls drew the attention of the other cyclopes who stomped their way to the shore and would have killed the humans but for the motivated rowing of the Trojans. After they made port at Drepanum, Aeneas lost his beloved father to death, something none of the prophecies about Troy's future had prepared him for.

Aeneas' adventures next took him to the shores of Carthage in north Africa. It was ruled by Dido. Finally, Aeneas would understand the cryptic prophecy he had heard in Little Troy – that Juno, of all the gods, was the one to placate now. Juno, it turns out, loved Dido and Carthage, and the goddess even stored her chariot and weapons in that kingdom. Her love was returned in Carthage, and Dido was building Juno a huge temple.

Juno had heard a prophecy that a man like Aeneas would destroy Carthage. Pious Aeneas, the man who secured his household gods before running for his life, virtuous Aeneas had no intention of undoing a queen and ruining a great city.

And yet he did.

By this time, it had been many years since the abject defeat of Troy. The Trojans were trying, against all odds, to reach the western shores of

Italy. They had skirted around Sicily, encountered Charybdis. They had said the right prayers. They were good rowers.

Still, Juno didn't want them in Carthage. She went to the kingdom of Aeolus, god of winds. This is the same god to whom Ulysses applied for winds to return to Ithaca. Humbly, Aeolus obeyed Juno when she asked that he kick up a terrible storm to rout the Trojan fleet.

The sky above their ships darkened, the sea raged. Aeneas crumpled at the knees and implored heaven for mercy. Men who died on the beaches of Troy or in its burning town were exactly four times luckier than he, he shouted at the heavens. He wished he had died at the hands of the great Greek warrior Diomedes.

Three ships were dashed on the rocks. Aeneas was within sight of a ship whose captain was thrown overboard by the force of the wind and waves. The captain's ship soon followed and was swallowed by the sea. All around, humans were struggling in the chop, their treasured possessions floating nearby.

The savagery was so raw that Neptune rose above the waves to inquire what madness was disturbing his oceans. As soon as he thought of it, the seas calmed, the winds died, and the sky cleared. Light was restored to the daytime. Seven Trojan ships, survivors of that storm, found a port and landed in north Africa.

They made land and immediately started drying corn that had been drenched in salt water while Aeneas climbed a nearby mountain to see where they were. A herd of deer was nearby, so he shot seven of them – one for each of his surviving fleet – and carried them down to his band of wanderers. They paired this feast with a gift of wine that had survived the storm. Aeneas put on his game face and cheered them on.

'You've survived the cyclops and Charybdis! This is nothing! And the gods will make it up to us! I'm sure of that', was approximately how he tried to rally them. But he was working against his own anxiety. All of them were worried about friends they had lost and whether any could have survived the storm. Aeneas was missing several good friends: Orontes, Amycus, Gyas, and Lycus.

Far above, in the heavens, Jupiter was surveying his earthly resources. He had turned his attention to the battered Trojans when

Venus approached him. She reminded him of his promise – The Trojans would be the founders of a great city in Italy.

Jupiter smiled and reassured her that this was god working in mysterious ways. Trojan greatness was tied to Venus by fate. No mere shipwrecks could alter that. Aeneas would tame the savages of western Italy, build cities, and impose laws. The future reign of Ascanius, our hero's son, was a fixed point in space and time, Jupiter assured Venus.

Once the savages had been subdued, Aeneas would rule for three years, Ascanius for thirty, and three hundred years later, Romulus would be born, Jupiter continued. Romulus would officially found Rome. A line of kings, named Julius, would descend directly from Aeneas' pious loins. And they would take their name from Ascanius, whose other, Trojan name was Iulius.

And that is how Virgil drew a direct line from the noble and goddess-born Trojan remnant to the iron-fisted Roman governing machine.

Mercury descended on wings to Dido's palace to ensure that the Trojans would receive hospitality when they arrived. Meanwhile, Venus disguised herself as Diana with a cinched up dress and bow and quiver. She met Aeneas in the woods. He could tell at once that she was not a human, and asked if she were Apollo's sister, but she insisted that she was just a local Libyan girl, and this was how they dressed.

She pointed him in the direction of Queen Dido of Carthage. Dido's brother had murdered her beloved husband, Venus explained. But her husband visited her in a dream and told her where there was a hidden cache of gold and silver. She should run from her murderous brother and establish a new kingdom far from him, her husband's ghost said. She located the treasure and did as the ghost urged. Dido had bravely established this town in north Africa with its fine citadel, cobbled streets, theatre, and temple.

Venus then hid Aeneas in a mist so that he was invisible as he walked into the busiest part of the city. He made his way to Juno's temple. There, he was surprised and dismayed to see temple paintings that commemorated the Trojan war in stages. It brought home that they had been wandering for *seven* years. The scenes of that war brought him to tears, but he cheered himself with the thought that fame might bring his people a measure of safety.

It must have been weird to see the painting of Troilus fighting Achilles and losing – badly. Aeneas remembered his young colleaguc's death. After losing the fight, he was dragged behind a horse-drawn chariot on his back, his dead body tangled up in the reins. Did Aeneas think that it could so easily have been he, himself, who had lost to the great Achilles? Finally, he spotted himself in one of the paintings. There he was, mixed up with a crowd of Greeks on the battlefield.

While Aeneas was quietly reliving the Trojan war, his lost comrades, people he thought were dead, were making their way to the temple where Dido had arrived. Her throne sat in the temple and she took her seat there. She was well guarded by a military escort rich in spears. Aeneas continued to wonder at the miracle that had saved the doomed Trojans. Here they were, safe in Carthage. He watched as his fellow traveller, Ileonius, approached Dido's throne and asked for help.

He identified himself as Trojan and quickly clarified that they had landed there as a result of a terrible storm. They were not there to make war, Ileonius assured her, but they did need new oars, so he would need to cut some trees. He asked only for the freedom of the city and mentioned that his party had been denied access at the border by threats of war. Not knowing that Aeneas was in that very temple, listening, he said that their leader might be lost at sea or dead; they did not know where he was.

Dido made what must be one of the earliest jokes equating light with intellect. 'When the sun god makes his journey across the sky, he doesn't skip us here in Libya. We know who the Trojans are', was roughly her first response.[4]

Did Aeneas know he was still enshrouded in a mist created by Venus? It doesn't matter, for, in that moment, she removed it and made him radiant. His eyes and hair shone. He was a beautiful man. Every eye turned toward him, and he spoke to Dido, thanking her for her compassion. He pledged never to forget her kindness; he could never repay her, so he hoped the gods would reward her generosity. Then he greeted the men he thought he had lost.

Dido literally replied, 'Are you *that* Aeneas?'[5] in Shadi Bartsch's wonderfully down-to-earth translation. Then she told the assembled visitors to make themselves welcome. She led Aeneas to her palace, having first ordered that hundreds of goats, sheep, bulls, and boars be sent to the beach to feed the sailors who had stayed with the ships. This not only assuaged their hunger but also gave them the wherewithal to make sacrifices of gratitude to the gods who gave them safe passage.

Aeneas sent his friend Achates to fetch his son and several expensive items that had been saved from burning Troy, notably a robe, edged with gold, that had belonged to Helen, a crown inlaid with gems, a pearl necklace, and a sceptre. These would be fitting gifts for Dido, he believed.

For her part, Venus plotted. In her mind, there was no price too high to save Aeneas and usher him to his destiny as the founder of Rome. Gracious Dido, generous Dido, beloved of her people, organised, thoughtful, a great administrator, a multitasker, this great queen was utterly disposable in Venus' thoughts.

Dido might well have fallen in love with Aeneas on her own, but an ordinary, nourishing, whole grain kind of love was not what Venus had in mind. She wanted Dido out of her mind, obsessed. Then she would do anything, with no thought for her own safety much less her kingdom.

And that was the kind of thing her son Cupid was good at. So Venus located Cupid and asked him to do a swap. She would put the real Ascanius into a deep sleep and hide him in a shrine, while Cupid posed as Ascanius and got close enough to Dido to infuse her with a reckless passion. Cupid agreed; by removing his wings and practicing Ascanius' walk, he transformed himself into Aeneas' son. Loaded with the gifts Aeneas ordered, Cupid entered Dido's palace.

Hundreds of people sat down to the feast that Dido threw in honour of her visitors. In their midst, Dido took Cupid on her lap, thinking he was a boy, thinking he was Aeneas' son. Sitting there, doing his slow, insidious work, Cupid slowly erased her first, murdered husband from Dido's heart, a heart unused for years. There was no vulgar stabbing with an arrow in Virgil's poem, just a slow, deadly virus, one that self-replicated until the virtuous queen was quite undone.

Dido asked to hear Aeneas' story. Over the course of a few hours, he told her and the assembled guests of the Greek horse, the fall of Troy, his escape, and his wanderings in the Mediterranean. Over the next few days or weeks, Dido nursed her crush. Virgil likens her to a deer that has received a mortal shot. She wanders the woods for days in terrible pain, not fully understanding that her injury is fatal.

Dido confided in her sister, Anna Perana. Anna sensibly told Dido to marry Aeneas if she liked him. After all, Anna noted, she had refused suitors all over the known world. She had even rejected Iarbas, a Berber king who had offered her the protection of his great tribe. Anna also pointed out that there were warlike people surrounding the new city of Carthage and that Aeneas' army would offer some much-needed protection.

Dido was at war with herself. She had sworn to stay faithful to her dead husband. In her mind, therefore, her love for Aeneas was 'sinful'. Even though she had been robbed of free will, Virgil agreed with her on this point. It was too late, however, to avoid this obsession. Where the gods have determined to sacrifice one human's welfare for another, there is no recourse.

Perhaps the most disturbing scene in Dido's story takes place in Juno's temple. Anna and Dido had already sacrificed several fine sheep, then Dido wandered among the gory sacrifices, trying to read prophecies in the splattered guts of dead animals. If we needed new proof that sexual attraction can unspool a woman's very fabric, Dido gave us that. Formerly a visionary lawmaker and architect, she was now the pawn of superstition.

Thinking that her sacrifices and prayers were still not enough to provide the desired outcome, she added new material, doubling the offerings. Imagine the powerful Dido walking between the altars, adding loaves of bread, salt, and wine to the shrines of Ceres and Apollo, but especially Juno. That goddess certainly *meant* to protect Dido. But she could not.

When the Trojans arrived, Carthage was thriving. There was plenty of new construction, the city borders were well protected, trade was brisk. Dido had kept her citizens productive and happy. Now, the engineers were nowhere to be seen, building had stopped, soldiers did no drills, the harbour and borders were left unguarded and unreinforced. Bartch's translation of the *Aeneid* shows readers a crane rising to the sky, but at a standstill, and unfinished walls.[6]

The Trojans and Dido's people went hunting at dawn. By prior agreement with Venus, Juno churned up a storm so violent that Aeneas and Dido sought the refuge of a cave. Juno's plan was to 'marry' the two there. They would have sex, surely, then Aeneas would have to stay in the new Carthage and make it strong. Juno even assured Venus that Aeneas could rule over Dido. It was a win/win for everyone, Juno explained.

The storm came, Dido and Aeneas met outside the cave. The nymphs howled in the distance. A lightning bolt lit up the sky. Juno and her devout follower Dido took these as signs that the two were united in wedlock. Dido withheld the strength of her passion no longer.

At this point in the *Aeneid,* Virgil takes a break from the narrative and gives his readers a vivid description of the goddess called by many names: Pheme, Fama, Fame, and, in Bartsch's translation, Rumour. Yes, the same earthly goddess that destroyed mental health on Lemnos. As soon as Dido consummated her passion for Aeneas, Rumour took to the streets of Libya – running:

> Rumour, swiftest of all evils; she thrives
> on strength and gains strength as she goes. At first,
> she's small and scared, but soon she reaches to the skies,
> her feet still on the ground, her head hidden in clouds.

She was a specifically Roman god, one whose pretty face is fame with honour and whose ugly face is a smear of gossip. She ran so fast that we know little about her. She may have been the last of the titans, born of Gaia's rage at the new gods. That origin would make her a creature of earth, like the one-eyed cyclops, an ancient thing. She carried the story of Dido's unsanctioned passion through the streets. Her speed was the seemingly supernatural speed of gossip.

> She's fast of foot and fleet of wing, a huge
> horrific monster. Under all her feathers lurk
> . . . as many watching eyes and tongues,
> as many talking mouths and pricked-up ears.[7]

This Rumour never sleeps, she perches on rooftops and towers, frightening whole cities, and she makes little distinction between the truth and fiction. Made up gossip is just as good for business. The gossip about Dido was partly true – she shared a bed with Aeneas. And it was partly false – the two of them had lost all ambition and were neglecting their kingdoms while revelling in luxury.

Rumour had achieved her goal when word of the affair reached King Iarbas, Dido's former suitor. Dido had refused him when she was in her right mind. He was predictably furious. He had offered her protection. It now appeared that Dido *needed* protection, especially from him.

Iarbas was a savage, but not a godless one. He was the son of Hammon – Jupiter's African alter ego – and a raped nymph. He had built a hundred altars to Jupiter, and altar flames burned throughout his desert kingdom. Now he prayed to Jupiter, while angrily clutching one of these shrines.

To hear Iarbas tell it in his prayer, Dido had deeply offended him. He had offered her marriage. She could have shared in his vast desert kingdom. Now, NOW, she had given herself to some refugee. Though the comparison wasn't really apt, he likened Aeneas to Paris, a lazy wife stealer of indifferent piety.

That got Jupiter's attention. He looked down on Carthage, then sent Mercury with a message: Venus had promised the Trojan remnant a great future, and this was not it. If Aeneas were not ambitious for himself, should he not consider his son's future? Carthage was not an empire. It was barely a city; even Iarbas despised its small size. Where were the great, bloody battles that the gods were looking forward to? Bartsch transcribes it beautifully:

> He was to rule an Italy
> of war-cries, pregnant with an empire; to start a race
> from Teucer's ancient blood, and control the world.[8]

Mercury put on his winged sandals and shot down to Carthage. There he found Aeneas innocently overseeing the construction of new homes and defences as you might expect from the leader of a displaced people. A royally purple garment that Dido had woven herself sat on his shoulders.

This was the moment Mercury chose to read him the riot act. The god mercilessly mocked Aeneas for building up Carthage into a great city, for being a 'good husband', and generally bailing on his manifest destiny. He underlined this lecture by noting that he had been sent by Jupiter, king of all the gods, who was terribly disappointed.[9]

Mercury pretty much had Aeneas by showing up. The winged sandals would have given away his identity with little need for introductions. Our hero was terrified. His hair stood on end, not for the first time in this journey. Who knew the gods could be that angry with a widow and widower settling down together to protect their people? Okay! Okay!

There was no choice. They had to go to western Italy, where they had been told to go – twice now. Aeneas sent men to the harbour to ready the ships. The other Trojans had orders to head down to the beach. To his credit, Aeneas did consider how best to break the news to Dido. He did not intend to leave without saying good-bye. But Dido saw the preparations, and she confronted him with the worst assumptions, calling him a traitor, accusing him of trying to make a covert getaway.

Dido and Aeneas held different points of view on their marriage. Aeneas' point of view was that he wasn't in a marriage. He had never raised a marriage torch or said the words of a contract. He did not wish to be unkind, however.

He pleaded with Dido to see his problem. He described the visit from Mercury that had set his hair on end. Jupiter's orders were very clear; they could not be ignored without deep offence to the most powerful Olympians. And finally he admitted that he would prefer to stay there with Dido. But his fate was not in his own hands. That is what it means to have an explicit destiny.

This was Dido's chance to reach out the hand of eternal friendship. But she was a bundle of nervous pride and thwarted lust. Her obsession with Aeneas had taken hold of her like a pathology or an addiction. She raged at him. He was a liar! His mother wasn't Venus! Mercury hadn't visited him! She took him in as a beggar! The gods had no sense of justice! He would be shipwrecked! Her name would be the last word he would say, going down with his ship! *She would see him in hell!*

Meanwhile, the Trojans were motivated. The anger of the gods may have seemed a little remote to the servants and farmers who had followed Aeneas to Africa. But the anger of *Dido* and everyone who was loyal to her was real enough.

They worked at a brisk pace, cutting down tree branches and making oars, rolling huge containers of grain to the ships. Dido saw them scurrying to leave. It was killing her. Could Cupid not have poisoned her with a kinder, gentler love, one that could morph to friendship and diplomacy? No! That would not be tragic enough. A great destiny calls for a great sacrifice, right? If someone triumphs, someone must also grovel.

Dido asked her sister Anna to plead with Aeneas, and she made several attempts to make him stay. But Aeneas stood firm in his resolution to sail on. Dido did have options. She could still marry an African king. She could sail with Aeneas. She rejected both these avenues out of pride.

Instead, she raised a huge bonfire and put most of her lover's clothes and any weapons left behind in the fire to feed it. After several more lamentations, she fell on a sword. Iris swept down to earth, leaving a rainbow in her wake, and collected the poor queen's soul. As they sailed away from Carthage, the Trojans saw the city burning. They did not know who had started the fire. Aeneas would not know of Dido's death until he saw her in the underworld.

They were blown off course and landed in Sicily where Aeneas' good friend, Acestis, reigned. It was time for games, an ancient Greek and Roman tradition that kept men fighting fit. The ship race and foot race went off smoothly. Then Aeneas called for boxing.

The fighter, Dares, volunteered but the rest of the assembled men remembered when Butes, a man known for his large size, had gone up against Dares and died on the yellow beach at Troy, near Hector's burial place. No one volunteered to fight Dares, especially after he threw a few air punches.

Dares was about to declare himself the victor by default. He walked over to the prizes Aeneas had set out and claimed them, since there was no opponent. But Acestes goaded his friend Entellus into fighting. In Bartsch' wonderful translation, Acestes 'raked Entellus with harsh words' about his failure to give Dares a run for his money.[10]

Entellus, a prize fighter, said his blood was sluggish with age, but then he threw a couple of terrifying leather gloves into the fighting ring. Aeneas examined them and felt their weight. They were made with the leather of seven bulls and reinforced with lead and iron. They were the gloves Eryx had worn when he boxed with Hercules. They were a reminder that Eryx had been Entellus' fighting instructor. They were badly stained with brains and blood.

Entellus could see that the gloves gave him an advantage, perhaps when the spectators gasped as one, so he offered to exchange them for gloves of Aeneas' choice. Bartsch refers to our hero as 'Father Aeneas' as he carefully puts gloves of the same weight on both contestants. This was a game, after all, among friends. They weren't fighting for territory.

Imagine a young fighter going up against Ali. The younger fighter has the fast feet; the older scares people just with the sight of his naked chest and shoulders. Entellus spent the first round of the fight rooted in place, like an old tree, twisting and dodging to avoid Dares' blows. Entellus did not want to kill Dares.

In fact, he hoped to end the fight by bringing down one powerful blow on his young opponent. But he missed. The agile Dares darted right out of the way, and Entellus lost his balance and went crashing to the ground like a toppled oak.

That was humiliating, and when he arose, he was not in the same charitable frame of mind. He was 'berserk with bitter rage'.[11] Perhaps he was mad at himself. Perhaps he was enraged at the inevitable limitations that old age imposes, even on the most resilient of us. In any event, his anger was directed at Dares, and Dares was now in trouble.

When Entellus had regained his stance, he rained blows down on his opponent who danced all around the ring, trying to evade him. Dares was spitting teeth and blood clots by the time Aeneas decided to intervene.

He pulled the young man out of the fight. Somehow, Aeneas knew exactly the right thing to say that would save Dares' pride. The gods had joined their strength to Entellus. It would be madness to continue this fight. Dares conceded the fight and his friends took him, trembling, back to the ship.

Aeneas had set aside a bull as a prize for the winner. Entellus brought his powerful fist down on the bull's head and killed it instantly. But his rage was fading. As the bull was twitching its last, Entellus dedicated it calmly to his tutor Eryx and asked that this bull's life be accepted as a substitute for Dares'. Then he announced his formal retirement from boxing.

An archery contest followed. Then came the jewel in the games – Ascanius and other young men donned full armour, mounted their steeds and performed a number of equestrian tricks for their assembled families. They made the horses dance and move in circles and patterns that delighted their audience.

It was quite the recital, and their parents were enormously proud. As parents do, they were looking for inherited traits. In their talented and agile children, they saw both themselves and the past generations.

Virgil takes a beat to tell us their futures. Atys was a beloved friend of Ascanius. He would father the formidable Atii clan. Ascanius would be the ancestor of Romulus whose image would be stamped on Roman coins.

But Juno was now angry with the Trojans over the death of Dido, the loss of Carthage, and the delightful temple that Dido had been building, specifically for Juno. She was flying over and saw them – so happy at the accomplishments of their children, so hopeful for the future. How dare they!

She sent Iris to sow discord among some Trojan women who were memorialising Anchises in ceremonies on the beach. Iris disguised herself as one of their number – an old Trojan woman named Beroe who had lost her entire family to age, sickness, and war. Disguised as this respected widow, she wandered among the Trojan women, lamenting their seven years of futile wandering.

Why did they have to keep travelling? This was a nice place! Why couldn't they stop here! She claimed to have had a dream in which the priestess Cassandra told them to settle here. The irony here is that Cassandra, herself, was not believed, though her prophecies were always exactingly true. Here was a fraudulent prophecy falsely attributed to Cassandra, but it *was* believed.

Pyrgo, an elderly nurse, one who had cared for King Priam's children, pointed out that the imposter's eyes blazed too bright to be a mortal. Furthermore, Pyrgo asserted, she had just come from Beroe's bedside, and that woman was sick. She had sent her regrets for not being able to honour Anchises at this memorial.

Still disguised as an old Trojan widow, Iris picked up a torch, lit it at a nearby altar and threw it at one of the docked ships. Then she dropped her disguise and flew through the sky, creating a rainbow in her wake.

Yes, she had captured the mood of many women there at the beach. They had not seen the horse parade; the tone of their gathering was one of unhappy resignation. Soon, many women were throwing burning branches and homemade rockets at the fleet. The fires raged so hard that the men on the games field saw the smoke rising.

Ascanius, already mounted on a horse, was first in the race to the ships. And the first to see them burning. He reproached the women. How had they turned on their own people? How had they destroyed their own hopes for the future, he asked them. The women scattered and hid in nooks along the beach. Their Juno-inspired madness had deserted them, and now they understood the scope of what they had done.

Aeneas caught up to Ascanius. The Trojans did what they could to douse the flames, but they had no fire truck with cans of water and foam under pressure. So the flames continued to destroy the ships' frames.

The tidal wave of self-pity that Aeneas had been holding back broke free when he saw his burning fleet. He tore the clothes off his body and called to Jupiter to save his ships or kill all of the Trojans. Either by lightning or by drowning, they were better off dead. In answer, a heavy rain kicked up and extinguished the flames.

They had lost four ships, the hulls and frames too damaged to be seaworthy. But those damaged ships were not the only things that would be left in Sicily. Aeneas finally took a survey and identified the Trojans that wished to stay with Acestes and help him build a version of Troy there.

Quite a few weary travellers elected to stay, with Aeneas' blessing. Acestes agreed to let them settle and build a city next to his. Aeneas ploughed lines in the earth to mark off the city limits and individual estates. They would call this new land Acesta, in honour of their extremely gracious host. One part of the new city would be called 'Ilium', the other part 'Troy'.

But there were other weary Trojans who had not lost hope in Aeneas' dream. The grandeur of what they could accomplish was still real to them. They didn't have to guess their destinies, or make them up on the spot, as most people must do. The gods had personally instructed them. They had a clearly spelled out, glorious future. How many people have that?

So, when they struck the oars again, it was western Italy or bust. Aeneas' people, the ones who still held fast to the dream, were strong and brave. Their faith was unshakeable. They believed in the benevolence of their gods . . . still, but, more importantly, they believed in themselves and their leader. Venus negotiated with Neptune to give these Trojan ships fair weather and, at last, they landed at the bay of Cumae.

Aeneas sought the reputedly mad Sibyl as he had been commanded. She was in a cave near Apollo's temple. The news from Sibyl was not good. Sure, they were on dry land right now and the sailing was behind them. They *would* make a settlement in Italy, but it would not come without conflict and hard work. She saw wars and bloodshed in their future.

Sibyl also told him that he could visit his dead father in the Elysian Fields if he first located and broke off a golden branch of a tree belonging to Proserpina, queen of the underworld. This branch was the ticket to Hades, and he would not be able to see his father again without it.

On his return to the ships, Aeneas discovered that an old friend of Hector's, one Misenus, was dead. He was a talented bugler, and he had delighted, briefly, in making music along the cliffs. He played so well that Triton, who also plays a horn, took it as a challenge to the gods and drowned him among the rocks near the beach. Virgil is brave enough to call it an unjust death.

While the Trojans mourned the loss of Misenus, Aeneas muttered something like a prayer that the golden branch he needed would show itself. Two doves landed near him. They were Venus' birds, and he knew that they would guide him. They flitted from branch to branch, feeding, and he followed them until he came to Avernus, the stinking mouth of the underworld.

The doves landed on a tree, and there it was – the golden branch – glimmering from within a crowd of green leaves. It broke off easily in Aeneas' hand, as it was enchanted to do. Sybil had assured him that another branch would grow in its stead – in time for the next heroic mortal who cared to brave the afterlife before his time.

Sibyl led Aeneas through her cave to the land of Dis, an unhappy place where hunger, old age, fear, and poverty were all personified. Then Aeneas had to cross a gauntlet of monsters – centaurs, gorgons, harpies, chimerae. He was terrified and drew his sword, but Sibyl told him these monsters were mere phantoms. They could not hurt him.

They moved on to the swirling waters of Acheron where Virgil gives us the most amazing, detailed picture of the underworld, by way of Shadi Bartsch's translation. There lay the 'sluggish depths of Cocytus and Styx', two rivers of Hades. Aeneas laid eyes on Charon, death's ferryman, whose tattered clothing stank. He was an ancient immortal, but an immortal, nonetheless. Bartsch describes him as possessing 'the green and raw old age of gods'.[12]

Dead souls, looking like their living selves, crowded around the bank of the Cocytus. They were waiting to be ferried across to their proper destination. But some of them were unburied, and Charon would not accept them on his boat. He could be seen shoving them back onto the sand with the same primitive pole that he used to drive his vessel.

There was an end point to the torture of a soul, however, in Virgil's underworld. After waiting on the shores for a hundred years, these unburied shades would finally be accepted onto Charon's dinghy. Then they would take their places among the other mostly unhappy ghosts.

Charon put up an argument when he saw two living beings attempting to cross the river. Sybil answered him bluntly. Aeneas, true born son of Venus, was here to see his father. She cited several other heroes who had been to hell and back, Hercules and Theseus, among them. Then, knowing that the gods don't really recognise the authority of precedent, she produced the golden branch from within her clothes. Upon seeing the branch, Charon calmed his fury and poled them across.

Their path was blocked by Cerberus, the three headed hellhound. Sybil, who proved a highly competent guide despite her crazy reputation, had provisioned herself with a piece of bread, carefully treated with wine and drugs. All three famished canine throats seized on that snack, and the beast slumped unconscious to the floor.

Aeneas saw many people he recognised; fellow fighters in the recent war were there. He found Dido, or she found him. He wept and attempted to make peace with her. She would not speak to him. She only stared daggers. But in the end, Virgil did not have the heart to prolong her miseries, even in hell. She left Aeneas and returned to her husband, Sychaeus, who shared her love and pain in the afterlife.

Perhaps the most shocking revelation of the underworld was Deiphobus's tale of how Troy had *really* been lost. Back in the days when Troy was under Greek siege, Helen's Trojan husband, Paris, had been killed. It was unthinkable – at least for the future Romans – that a woman of Helen's beauty would remain a widow. It was always safer for the able-bodied men of the population to keep her married so they didn't have to fight over her.

Oh, wait, they were already fighting over her. And it didn't help her leverage that she was a jumped up, foreign freeloader; at least that's how many members of Priam's family would have seen her. After Paris' death, she held about the same status as a slave.

The marriage to Deiphobus, Paris' brother, was forced on her, according to some sources. Deiphobus did not get much time to enjoy married life, however. Helen faked a Bacchic frenzy on the day that the horse appeared on the beach. She knew that it harboured Greek fighters, Deiphobus implied.

A Bacchic frenzy basically looks like a woman who is one drink over the line and now thinks she can talk to god. Singing, dancing, loud praying and chanting were all symptoms. Helen's fraudulent ecstasy inspired the Trojan citizens to drag that huge wooden and titanium horse up to the citadel. Then, from the Acropolis, she shone a torch, signalling to the Greek fleet that it was safe to sail back.

While her third husband was asleep, she removed all the weapons from the house, including the sword that Deiphobus kept under his pillow. Then she threw open the door of their home to Ulysses and Menelaus. Those two didn't just kill the sleeping Deiphobus, they mutilated him dramatically, slicing his nose, mangling his body, disfiguring his hands and face, tearing off his ears. He still bore these marks of disfigurement in Hades.

Helen betrayed the Trojans to the Greeks to guarantee her safety, Deiphobus asserted. It was a shocking story because in so many versions of the Trojan War and its aftermath, Helen has absolutely no agency. Now, Aeneas came to find out, she had all the agency. It's like finding out that a nun is the serial killer.

By this time, it was past noon, and Sibyl, who *must* have done this before, warned Aeneas that they must complete this journey and return to the world of the living before night fell. Deiphobus excused himself, telling Aeneas, 'Be luckier than me'.[13]

Aeneas' underworld was similar, but not identical to Ulysses'. Virgil wanted the world's heroes to enjoy the eternity of the soul. So he designed the underworld with sections: Tartarus for the wicked people and Elysium for those who lived decently, obeying their gods and the laws of the land.

Pious Aeneas would never see Tartarus, in this life or the next. So Sibyl summarised it for him. People who hated their own close family members, betrayed their masters, started infighting, committed fraud, or hoarded money without setting some aside for family members were all there, she said.

There was no one punishment in Tartarus. The punishments were tailored to the criminals. When Sibyl had finished explaining hell to Aeneas, they ventured into the realm of Proserpina where Aeneas symbolically sprinkled himself with fresh water and laid the golden branch on her threshold.

Aeneas saw many Trojans that had fought on his side in the war against the Greeks. They would have liked to have more time with him. He also saw Greeks that he had fought. But they were no threat to him now. Aeneas had put war into perspective, and now these enemies seemed like the shadows they had always been. They 'raised a weak war-cry that mocked their gaping jaws'.[14]

This is a pivotal moment in Aeneas' journey. He could see the futility of war. Winners and losers go to the same place. At the end of the day, a fighter can't build anything until he puts down his weapons. At least that's the lesson Aeneas should have learned.

As all mortals who visit Hades do, Aeneas had a specific mission. His father had haunted him in dreams. There was unfinished business here. Anchises lived in Elysium's fields of joy, the closest thing that the Romans had to heaven. Virgil put the poets, musicians, and priests in these fields. Orpheus was there, playing his seven-string lyre. Aeneas also saw Dardanus, Troy's founder.

Aeneas found Anchises in a valley. The son wept, of course, and tried three times to hug his father. But Anchises was a spirit without form. Though he looked tangible, there was no matter to seize on.

The scene in Anchises' Elysium was very similar to that last happy day in Sicily when Ascanius led the young men in a horse and armour show. Anchises spent his days with other souls who had enjoyed raising and racing horses when they were alive. As residents of the underworld, they still lived with horses, and raced their chariots against each other. Every day was a game they loved to play.

Anchises explained that Elysium was not the final resting place for any of the dead. After a thousand years, they would cross the river of forgetting, Lethe, and be reincarnated as earthly humans. The two of them could see the Lethe river from where they stood. In fact, there were souls loitering near that river, waiting for their rebirth. After a millennium, they longed to see the sun again.

And then Anchises revealed why he had summoned Aeneas to Elysium. He pointed to a young man learning on a spear with no point, waiting. *Waiting to be born*. That, Achises explained, would be Aeneas' son Sylvius, born to him in old age, from his future wife Lavinia. Through Sylvius, Aeneas' line would rule Italy for ages. He would be a father and a king of kings.

Anchises pointed out other illustrious descendants: Procas, Capys, Numitor, Romulus, and Silvius Aeneas. Eventually, Anchises referenced Augustus Caesar, drawing a straight line between the displaced Trojans and the great emperors of Rome.

All these names would have thrilled the Roman readers of Virgil's time because they were historic figures, not merely fictitious ones. It was like when Rosa Parks turns up in a science fiction show. With that chapter, Virgil fulfilled his mission to give the Augustan regime, of which our poet was a citizen, a prestigious back story.

Aeneas exited the underworld through the gates of sleep. Then he returned to his ships and his people. Neptune helped them out by giving them a gentle, steady wind. They passed the island of Circe, somewhat fearfully, without landing. But they could hear the roars of lions, wolves, bears, and wild boars that had formerly been men – transfigured by Circe's magic.

And then they found the place where the Tiber river dumps its yellow sand into the sea. The Tiber would be the river from which Rome expanded. The Trojans found the lands inhabited by

Latins, ruled by the wise and peaceful King Latinus. Latinus had lost his only son and now his only heir was his daughter, Lavinia. Many ambitious men hoped to be king, so she had no shortage of admirers. There was a frontrunner, Turnus, who had found favour with Lavinia's mother.

These Latins had received signs that the Trojans would settle here and transform the culture, well before Aeneas ever set foot in Italy. A sacred tree, precious to the king, had been infested with bees. When lighting an altar fire, Lavinia had been briefly engulfed in flames without coming to harm. This bizarre event was interpreted to mean that she would be famous, but would bring great conflict to her country.

Latinus was perplexed by these dramatic signs. He was an elderly man at this point and had no particular wish for drama. He did what any pious king would do – he consulted the divinities. This Latinus was the son of Faunus, a powerful rural god, greatly honoured by locals. To speak with Faunus, one needed to sacrifice sheep, lie on their skins, and dream. In these dreams, a religious man in good standing with the gods could hear their voices and ask questions.

Questions about the future weighed heavily on Latinus, so he sacrificed a hundred sheep at Faunus' shrine and lay down on their skins to sleep. In his dreams, he heard the gods tell him not to marry Lavinia to Turnus. The Trojans would become his sons, the gods told him, and they would raise the country to greatness. Keep in mind that the Trojans had multiple claims on Latium. Most importantly, the gods had ordained it to be their home. But they also believed that their ancestors had migrated to Asia and Troy from central Italy.

After docking their ships, the Trojans set out a nice picnic for themselves. As they did not have plates, they set pieces of flatbread on the ground and piled their food on the bread. They were famished, so after they ate their other food, they devoured the bread as well, and Ascanius joked that they were 'eating their tables'.

Do you remember the harpy's curse, dear reader? Aeneas remembered it. When his son dropped that one liner, Aeneas was struck speechless. He must have looked around and taken note of the day and time, the weather, the landscape. This was it, the land the gods had promised them, an 'end to exile'. Their seven-year journey was over. Aeneas stood and declared: 'I greet you, country owed to me by fate' and to his people, he said, 'This is our home, your native land'.[15]

This announcement transitioned seamlessly to prayer in which Aeneas thanked the gods for this settlement. Jupiter sent three loud thunderclaps to show his approval. A hundred Trojans walked to the palace of King Latinus with lavish gifts from the slender stock of treasures they had saved from their burning city.

The king greeted them hospitably. He knew who they were, of course. Who had not heard of the war for Troy and its brave survivors? Of course they could settle in these lands; they had the support of Latinus and all his people. His only condition was that he would like to shake Aeneas' hand in person.

He also mentioned that he had a daughter and, ahem, the gods had said she could not marry one of her countrymen. Casually, he gave them a gift of prize stallions, bedecked in gold chains and expensive fabrics. In turn, the Trojans promised eternal gratitude to Latinus and his kingdom. Aeneas' story really could have ended right there in chapter seven . . . but for Juno.

Juno was still seething with anger over the fall of Carthage and the death of Dido. She saw all of these lovey-dovey, getting along, making peace, negotiating win/win deals. It made her crazy.

You may have noticed that Juno liked to subcontract her dirty work. This time she visited hell and found Allecto, an ancient Fury with bat wings and snakes for hair. Juno commanded Allecto to 'undo the pact of peace and sow the crimes of war'.[16] The night goddess' first stop was not to Turnus, as you might expect, but to Queen Amata, Latinus' wife and Lavinia's mother. Allecto threw a snake at Amata, and it slid all over her, making her delusional and impulsive.

She had wanted Lavinia to marry Turnus, and now it seemed like a matter of life and death. She argued with her husband – the Trojans were pirates! Aeneas would marry Lavinia, then take her far away! Paris was a damn Trojan, and look what he started! Here was another Trojan getting ready to steal a princess!

She had no luck with her husband. The gods had spoken to him directly. No one with any common sense defies the direct orders of the gods. Amata faked a Bacchic frenzy in order to give a religious patina to her next actions. She hid Lavinia in a hillside forest, and cried loudly that none but the wine god Bacchus should have her.

Allecto then appeared to Turnus in a dream, having taken the form of an old priestess. But Turnus was a reasonable man – at least he had been up to that point. He called her 'auntie' and mocked her for catastrophising. Allecto bridled at the disrespect and turned herself into a huge flaming torch. Her snakes hissed at him. Then she threw, not a snake, but a firebrand that lodged in the poor man's chest and gave him an insatiable lust for violence and revenge. He arose from bed drenched in sweat and calling for weapons.

The pretext for war was well established now, but Allecto was not quite satisfied with her work She saw 'bright' Ascanius hunting with snares and dogs, and she remembered that there was a pet stag wandering by the river nearby. The king's gamekeeper had raised one of the forest deer as a pet for Sylvia, his daughter. The animal was so tame that it allowed her to brush him and put garlands in its antlers. Though it would wander the forest by day, it always came home to Sylvia at night.

With Allecto's help, Ascanius' dogs caught the scent of this deer and gave chase, barking joyfully. Ascanius, too, chased the deer, not knowing its emotional importance. You can hardly blame the boy. All those antlers; it would be a fine prize. But Ascanius was not yet that good at archery. 'Some god' guided his shaky arrow and drove it fast and deep into the stag's belly, killing it.[17]

Sylvia was devastated. Her father, Tyrrhus, grabbed his axe and summoned his fighters. Allecto blew a note on her bugle that was so loud and hellish, all the mothers of the city instinctively grabbed their children to keep them safe. Trojan fighters ran to Ascanius' side to defend him. Battle lines formed; the sides faced off. Before any older, wiser men could prevail on the jacked-up fighters, a single arrow flew through the air and killed Tyrrhus' oldest son, a young man named Amo.

Weapons flew and slashed, a war began in earnest. Brimming with pride, Allecto flew to heaven to report to Juno. She offered to spread the war to surrounding cities.

But Juno saw that Allecto had gone too far. Virgil gives us just the faintest hint that the queen of heaven felt threatened by such a display of power. She told Allecto to go home, she wasn't needed. Allecto's snakes hissed, but she complied with Juno's order.

Turnus quickly learned of the battle, and he incited his fellow Latins, declaring that the Trojans were there to replace him. The shepherds called Amo's death a murder. Women led by Amata added their voices to the others. A mob gathered outside Latinus' palace, demanding war.

But Latinus had not killed a hundred sheep in exchange for advice only to disregard that advice. He stood firm. And though Aeneas had not technically asked for Lavinia's hand, nor vice versa, their marriage was now a fixed point. Their son was in Elysium, waiting to be born, for gods' sake. *Rome was waiting.*

It was now inevitable that Aeneas would have to fight Turnus, despite the Trojan leader's best efforts to avoid a conflict. Yet, the Trojan men were depleted by shipwreck, exhausted from travel, and weakened by nutritional deficiencies. They were not fit to go up against Turnus' fresh-faced army alone.

They had acquired the help of a powerful local god, however. Tiber, spirit of the mighty Tiber river, had taken their part. Tiber appeared to our hero and told him to find Evander, a Greek settler who had built a city on a nearby hill. This city was Pallantium. Tiber declared he would guide Aeneas to this city along his river.

Aeneas chose two ships from his fleet to sail to Pallantium. Tiber calmed the river as they travelled. And it was near the river bank that Aeneas finally saw the snow-white pig with thirty piglets. He remembered Apollo's prophecy: When the white momma pig appears, 'that place will be your city, and an end to hardship'.

Well, it was not quite at an end. The Trojans would have to fight Turnus' army, Amata would commit suicide, and the conflict would only end when Aeneas killed Turnus in single combat. But Aeneas would at least have this comfort – he had followed the will of the gods until it hurt.

Evander was an old king in the *Aeneid,* but he was a culture hero to the Romans of the Augustan period. He had emigrated to Italy from the Arcadian region of Greece. The Romans of Virgil's time credited him with bringing the best of Greece – laws, myths, and an alphabet – to Rome.

Evander was the repository of Greek culture in pre-Roman Latium, but he lived simply and wore the skins of animals. He and his people followed Hercules. They remembered Hercules' defeat of Cacus, the fire-breathing giant that had terrorised their region.

Evander had his own, independent reasons for going up against Turnus. The latter had given sanctuary to a cruel leader, Mezentius, who was wanted for crimes against humanity. In fact, an army of thousands with ships attached had already been formed for the purpose of bringing Mezentius to justice. These troops were champing at the bit. But they had heard a prophecy telling them not to strike the oars until they had found a foreign leader. The gods had required them to wait for Aeneas to lead them.

Evander's advanced age came with mobility issues. He put the Trojans in charge of the combined fighting forces. But he had a son who was around the same age as Ascanius. This boy was Pallas.

Evander cherished Pallas, but you can't raise a hero by coddling him. So he sent Pallas to the battlefield to learn leadership and the arts of war from Aeneas. Many Latins and Trojans lost their lives in the battle for Lavinia and the kingdom that came with her. Pallas was one of those who was killed.

The gods were more or less equally divided over who should win. Juno favoured Turnus, who also had an immortal sister, Juturna. She disguised herself as a charioteer to help him in battle. Aeneas would always be a favourite with Venus and, indirectly, with Vulcan. For the war with Turnus, Venus begged Vulcan to make a suit of armour for her son, which he did.

Jupiter was supposed to be an impartial observer, but in the end he sided with the Trojans, asking his wife to quell her fury against them. He also chided Juno for giving too much authority to Juturna who had been dominating the battle. Juno agreed, finally, to stand back and interfere no further.

Aeneas was hit with an arrow from an unknown fighter on the Latin side, and it injured him badly. His men helped him off the field, but Venus didn't trust the camp doctor. She picked some dittany, a herb often associated with healing, and mixed it into a potion. She got the potion into the hands of the doctor who was treating her son. The herbal solution healed Aeneas completely and instantly. He arose from his sick bed, strong and radiant.

The conflict would be settled in single combat – Aeneas against Turnus. In this final encounter, no gods or goddesses guided their hands or added to their strength. It was just two mortal men, who could have been allies, and the strength they had in their core and arms. Turnus had a distracted moment, looking for his sister who had disappeared. In that moment, Aeneas saw his chance. He threw his spear, and it lodged deep in Turnus' thigh. Turnus crumpled to the ground and asked for mercy.

Pious Aeneas considered the wisdom of sparing Turnus and forming an alliance with his people. But then he saw Pallas' belt, the belt that previously had held his sword. After killing Pallas, Turnus had wrapped that belt around his shoulder – a souvenir of the time he killed Evander's son during his first battle. Outraged, Father Aeneas plunged his sword into Turnus' heart and killed him instantly.

The Triumph of Monotheism

We have disbelieved in the Roman gods for so many centuries, it can be difficult to remember that regular people believed in Jupiter as a divine being. Similarly, the ancients worshipped Juno, Diana, Minerva, Venus, and Mercury. They not only believed that these gods existed, but they also believed their gods could hear prayers and grant petitions. Fresh air shrines and temples were their churches. But belief in the new god, Jesus, was already crowding out belief in the Dei Consentes during Ovid's lifetime.

One obvious problem with the Roman gods is that they fail to provide a consistent moral compass. The *Metamorphoses* is sort of a bible for Roman belief; it compiles the narratives that form the basis for faith. But it is, equally, a scandalous text that the Victorians, centuries later, found morally reprehensible. The *Metamorphoses* is enormously entertaining. But it does not provide a guide to ethical behaviour. Nor do the works of most other ancient Roman writers.

Christianity, when it came along, provided that moral guidebook. It quickly displaced belief in multiple gods. The patriarchal nature of monotheism held great appeal for patriarchs. And they were the ones in position to determine what the rest of society would affirm.

Some scholars claim that it was the miracles of Christianity that made it so popular. Jesus performed quite a few of these, and his followers were known for magic, as well. But miracles and magic are in the very fabric of Roman myth. How many miracles did Medea perform to get Jason the golden fleece? How often did Jupiter throw a lightning bolt to end a violent conflict? How often did Venus manipulate events just by making somebody pretty? It seems a stretch to say that Christianity rose on miracles when miracles were the currency of the Roman gods.

The afterlife is another powerful incentive to belief. Christians offered their believers an eternity in heaven after a lifetime of sacrifices. But the Romans, too, believed that individual consciousness continued after death. When a character in Roman myth contemplates suicide, it is with the belief that life will continue in the conflict-free underworld. Virgil, following the example of Homer, even sectioned the afterlife so that the most virtuous and heroic men and women spent eternity in Elysium, a paradisal region within the underworld that features beautiful landscapes and endless recreation. Scholars who think that heaven was a Christian innovation are mistaken. The ancients already believed in a version of heaven, and someone who doesn't mind being called a heretic might think that Elysium is more fun.

Christianity developed as a sect within Judaism. Paul the Apostle is credited with spreading the faith beyond the Jewish community. This Paul started life as a high-ranking Pharisee in Jerusalem. His conversion experience looks a lot like something that could happen in Ovid's *Metamorphoses*. On the road to Damascus, he is struck by a bright light which temporarily blinds him. As he is writhing in pain and disbelief, the voice of god speaks to him, explaining that Christianity is the one true faith.

This miracle was enough to convert Paul and make him a proselyte. Where before he defended Judaism against this new, strange religion, now he spread it. He travelled and founded Christian colonies wherever he went. He became the first missionary.

We know of Paul exclusively through the New Testament, of which he was a major contributing author. It would be naive to credit him exclusively with the global expansion of Christianity, but scholars do seem to agree that Christianity was a grassroots system of belief. It moved slowly but inexorably, and on foot. It spread first amongst the farmers and workers, not the idle rich.

And maybe it wasn't about the miracles, per se, but about the kind of miracles. The miracles of polytheism revolved around the strong and brave. But this new religion offered solace and healing to the most vulnerable. The sick felt better, the lame walked, the hungry were fed. This egalitarianism – the notion that ordinary, unheroic people should be protected, not cast aside as rejects – was at the heart of early Christianity.

And then there were the blood sacrifices, seemingly required by the Dei Consentes. Even when poets like Ovid were madly substituting goats for female adolescents, blood sacrifice would not be an easy tradition for the poor. That ox was often the most valuable thing a family owned, and it was needed to plough a field. Christianity came along and said that thoughts and prayers were enough to honour god. In a Christian world, your daughters and working animals were a little safer.

Augustine of Hippo's life illustrates the transition from polytheism to Christianity in the fourth century *anno domini*. He was born to a Christian mother and a polytheist father who converted to Christianity on his deathbed. As a young man, Augustine rejected his mother's faith and flirted with Manichean belief, which combined several belief systems, both pagan and monotheistic.

But Augustine sought the kind of moral philosophy which could be seen in a believer's actions. When he met a Manichean bishop, he was so disappointed, he could not continue in the faith. Similarly, he did not find the transformation he sought in Neoplatonism. But in Ambrose of Milan, a Christian bishop, he found the inspiration he needed. Augustine became a Christian and later a bishop in Africa. By popular acclaim, he was declared a saint.

The Dei Consentes did not disappear; they were subsumed into metaphor. In Saint Augustine's writings, the Trojan gods represent the old, corrupt ways of pagan belief. The one true god triumphs over them. The multiple sackings of Rome in 390, 410, 455, 546, etc. mirror the overthrow of Roman religion and philosophy.

Saturnalia into Christmas

Amateur mythologists, especially, like to point out how Christmas draws a lot of imagery and customs from the Roman holiday, Saturnalia.

Like Christmas, Saturnalia offered a break from work during the bleakest part of the year. In a world that did not feature central heating, gas cooking, or overhead LED fixtures, your average pagan got a little frantic when the temperatures plummeted below zero. Snow and ice don't make things easier, even now.

Saturnalia, therefore, looked a lot like an illegal poker game wrapped in violence, and dipped in a thin sauce of religious justification. It was nominally a celebration and tribute to the god Saturn, who was already imprisoned by the Olympians, in the imaginations of Saturn's worshippers.

Saturnalia honours Saturn because he ruled over a long-defunct golden age. In Saturn's day, before the Olympians, food just offered itself to humans, and we didn't have to work so hard for calories. During winter food shortages, Roman farmers were nostalgic for that time in the world's history.

If you were a slave or serf, December was a dangerous time of year – no crops to bring in, no crops to thresh, no crops to plant. Not enough to do. Idle hands. It's an ideal time for a landowner massacre. What to do?

What early Roman farmers did was to liberate their slaves . . . for a week. It was an attempt to release the pressure off a steam engine that is going to blow. Saturnalia released the indentured to act on their natures. For the week of Saturnalia, they could go where they wanted, drink what they wanted, even offer some much needed feedback to their masters. Throughout the centuries of its observance, Saturnalia involved servants disrespecting masters, human sacrifice, partying, and drunkenness. Moderation gave way to excess until the Romans, in their enduring quest for order, reformed it into more of a state religion.

In a later, Christianised Rome, Saturnalia gave way to a holiday celebrating the birth of Jesus Christ. Though that god was not born in the darkest days of winter, Christmas eventually replaced Saturnalia, but not before appropriating many of Saturnalia's customs, especially gift giving, meat eating, and fire. The squandering of candles during Saturnalia's short days morphed into Christian rituals in which candles accompanied heartfelt prayers, often for lost loved ones. The Christmas tree is a direct import from Saturnalia. From the subordination of Saturnalia into Christmas, we see how one religion adapts and absorbs competing religions, making belief and custom serve economic purposes. Religion is used, and has always been used, to mollify the hardest-working labourers and reconcile otherwise terribly repressed populations to their fate. But people are often more attached to the rituals and fetishes of religion than to the belief itself. When one is trying to loosen the grip of a people on their gods, one must not too quickly ask them to release the icons and traditions of those gods. Safer to imbue the icon with a new meaning.

Mythology in the Renaissance and Beyond

The stories from ancient Rome persisted in literary forms and visual art as well. By Shakespeare's time – the late sixteenth and early-seventeenth centuries – Roman myth was already well debunked as a religion. But it provided the bard with beautiful settings and characters to play with. We have seen how *A Midsummer Night's Dream* resonates with imagery and characters from Ovid's writings. *Titus Andronicus, Julius Caesar, Anthony and Cleopatra,* and *Coriolanus* were also set in ancient Rome.

The poets of the Enlightenment – John Dryden, Alexander Pope, and Joseph Addison – believed that the ancient Roman texts were crude, but important. They set their hands to translating Ovid, elegantly. Dryden was so confident of his rhetoric that he 'improved' Ovid, embellishing and outright adding to the text as he went along.[1]

By the eighteenth century, Roman myth was becoming 'the classics', something to be taught in school. And perhaps a few public school teachers noticed the similarities between the Roman stories and those of Christianity. But they never encouraged too many comparisons.

In the Victorian period, mythology of all kinds became an important escape pod for poets and playwrights. Only in the aftermath of the Trojan War could Alfred Tennyson express his full longing for a life of endless inquiry and exploration.

In the twentieth century, T. S. Eliot referenced several ancient Roman characters in his poem, *The Wasteland*. In particular, Eliot liked to contrast the world of myth and magic with the dreary doings of modern life as in these lines:

> I Tiresias, though blind, throbbing between two lives,
> . . . can see . . . the evening hour that strives
> Homeward, and brings the sailor home from sea,
> the typist, home at tea time, clears her breakfast, lights
> Her stove, and lays out food in tins.[2]

In fact, the old gods never go away, not entirely. James Baldwin rewrote the stories of Prometheus, Jupiter, Neptune, Hades, Perseus, and Io in his book *Old Greek Stories* (in which he uses both Greek and Roman names for the Dei Consentes). In Baldwin's work, the ancient gods represent the deceitful power structure from which the poor and minorities are excluded.

The Roman myths survive in the imaginations of modern poets, artists, and filmmakers. The names Hercules, Venus, and Cupid resonate with cultural meaning even now. Everything changes. Stories fade into oblivion. But these ones haven't. Not yet.

Notes

Author's Note

1. Ovid, Publius. *The Fasti, Book 5*. The Theoi Texts Library. (Online: https://www.theoi.com/Text/OvidFasti5.html.)
2. Hejkuk, Julia Dyson. 'Ovid and Religion', in *A Companion to Ovid*. Peter E. Knox (ed.). Blackwell Publishing, 2009. p. 45.
3. Ovid, Publius. *The Fasti, Book 3*. The Theoi Texts Library. (Online: https://www.theoi.com/Text/OvidFasti3.html.)
4. Apuleius, Lucius. *The Golden Ass*. Sarah Ruden (trans.). New Haven: Yale, 2011. p. xii.
5. Farrell, Joseph. 'Apuleius and the Classical Canon'. Scholarly Commons, University of Pennsylvania, n.d., p. 1.

Introduction

1. Marlow, Christopher. *Plays of Christopher Marlowe*. London: Dent, p. 154.
2. Ovid, Publius. *The Fasti*. A. J. Boyle and R. D. Woodard (trans.). London: Penguin, 2000, p. 8.
3. Ovid, Publius. *The Metamorphoses*. David Raeburn (trans.). London: Penguin, 2004. p. 35.

PART I: THE ROYAL FAMILY

Chapter 1: Jupiter and Juno

1. Ovid, Publius. *The Fasti*. A. J. Boyle and R. D. Woodard (trans.). London: Penguin, 2000, pp. 119–121.

2. Ovid, Publius. *The Metamorphoses*. David Raeburn (trans.). London: Penguin, 2004, p. 35.

Chapter 2: Transformations

1. Ovid, *Metamorphoses*, p. 72.
2. Ovid, *Metamorphoses*, p. 15.
3. Ovid, *The Fasti*, pp. 95–98.
4. Ovid, *Metamorphoses*, p. 105.
5. Ibid., pp. 105–107.
6. Ovid, *Fasti*, pp. 76–77.
7. Ibid., p. 79.
8. Virgil., *Georgics*, p. 40.
9. Ovid, *Metamorphoses*, pp. 81–82.
10. Ibid., pp. 82–88.
11. Ibid., p. 102.
12. Ibid., pp. 99–104.
13. Ibid., pp. 429-431.
14. Ibid., pp. 28–33.

Chapter 3: The Lovers

1. Campbell, Caroline. Sandro Botticelli: Venus and Mars in Renaissance Florence. London: National Gallery, 2017. (https://www.youtube.com/watch?v=jNkHq6QXX30.)
2. Apuleius, Lucius. *The Golden Ass*. Sarah Ruden (trans.). New Haven: Yale, 2011. pp. 85–131.
3. Ovid, *Metamorphoses*, p. 383.
4. Ibid.
5. Ibid., pp. 382–385.
6. Ibid., p. 422.
7. Ibid., pp. 422–25.

PART II: THE HEROES

Chapter 4: Perseus

1. Ovid, *Metamorphoses*, p. 161.
2. Ibid., pp. 170–71.

3. Ogden, Daniel. *Perseus*. London: Routledge, 2008, p. 80.

4. Ovid, Publius. *Metamorphoses*, p. 177.

5. Ogden, *Perseus*, p. 145.

6. Scott, Walter. *Perseus*. New York: Little, 1892, p. 43.

Chapter 5: Hercules

1. Seneca, Lucius Annaeus. *The Ten Tragedies*. Frank Justus Miller (trans.). Complete Classics, n.d., pp. 8–9.

2. *Apollodorus' Library and Hyginus' Fabulae: Two Handbooks of Greek Mythology*. R. Scott Smith and Stephen M. Trzaskoma (trans.). Indianapolis: Hackett, 2007, p. 109.

3. Ovid, *Metamorphoses*, p. 342.

4. Ibid., p. 301.

5. Shakespeare, William. *Midsummer Night's Dream*. London: Bliss, Sands & Co., 1898, p. 6.

6. Ovid, *Metamorphoses*, p. 594.

7. Kingsley, Charles. *The Heroes*. Cambridge: Macmillan, 1859, p. lxii.

8. Seneca, *The Ten Tragedies*, pp. 119–121.

9. Ibid., p. 9.

10. Ibid., pp. 35–36.

11. Ibid., pp. 8–44.

12. Ibid., p. 264.

13. Ibid., p. 279.

14. Ibid., p. 298.

15. Ibid., p. 303.

16. Ibid., p. 307.

Chapter 6: Jason and Medea

1. Flaccus, Valerius. *The Argonautica*. J. H. Mozley (trans.). Cambridge: Harvard University Press, 1936, p. 273.

2. Ibid., p. 385.

3. Ibid., p. 397.

4. Ibid., p. 422.

5. Ibid., p. 431.

6. *Apollodorus' Library and Hyginus' Fabulae: Two Handbooks of Greek Mythology*. R. Scott Smith and Stephen M. Trzaskoma (trans.). Indianapolis: Hackett, 2007, p. 10.

7. Seneca, Lucius Annaeus. *The Ten Tragedies*. Frank Justus Miller (trans.). Complete Classics, n.d., p. 111.
8. Ibid., pp. 86–116.
9. *Apollodorus' Library and Hyginus' Fabulae*, pp. 107–08.

PART III: THE TROJAN WAR

Chapter 7: Preamble

1. Yeats, William Butler. 'Leda and the Swan', in *The Tower*. London: Macmillan, 1928, p. 51.
2. Tennyson, Alfred. 'Oenone', in *Poems*. London: Edward Moxon, 1833, pp. 60–64.
3. *Apollodorus' Library and Hyginus' Fabulae*, p. 129.
4. Ibid., p. 124.
5. Ibid., p. 128.
6. Cacoyannis, Michael. *Iphigenia*. City: Production Company, 1977.

Chapter 8: The Battlefield and the Horse

1. *Apollodorus' Library and Hyginus' Fabulae*, p. 133.
2. Ibid.
3. Virgil, Publius. *The Aeneid*. Shadi Bartsch (trans.). New York: Random House, 2021, p. 28.
4. Ibid., p. 27.
5. Ibid., pp. 33–34.
6. Ibid., p. 37.
7. Ibid., p. 50.
8. Ibid., p. 51.

Chapter 9: Aftermath

1. *Apollodorus' Library and Hyginus' Fabulae*, pp. 136–137.
2. Seneca, *The Ten Tragedies*, p. 199.
3. Ibid., p. 201.
4. *Apollodorus' Library and Hyginus' Fabulae*, p. 139.
5. Ibid., p. 140.
6. Ibid.

7. Ibid., p. 141.

8. Tennyson, Alfred. *The Poems of Alfred Tennyson*. Massachusetts: J. E. Tilton and Company. 1865. (https://www.google.com/books/edition/The_Poems_of_Alfred_Tennyson/rENDAQAAMAAJ?hl.)

Chapter 10: The Fall of Troy; The Rise of Rome

1. Virgil, Publius. *The Aeneid.* Shadi Bartsch (trans.). New York: Random House, 2021, p. 54.

2. Ibid., pp. 59–60.

3. Ibid., p. 63.

4. Ibid., p. 20.

5. Ibid., p. 22.

6. Ibid., p. 76.

7. Ibid., p. 79.

8. Ibid., p. 81.

9. Ibid., p. 82.

10. Ibid., p. 107.

11. Ibid., p. 109.

12. Ibid., p. 132.

13. Ibid., p. 139.

14. Ibid., p. 137.

15. Ibid., pp. 153–4.

16. Ibid., p. 160.

17. Ibid., p. 165.

Conclusion: The Triumph of Monotheism

1. Tissol, Garth. 'Dryden's Additions and the Interpretive Reception of Ovid', *Translation and Literature*, Vol. 13, No. 2, Versions of Ovid (Autumn, 2004), pp. 181–193. Retrieved through Jstor.

2. Eliot, T. S. 'The Waste Land', in *Modernism: An anthology*. Lawrence Rainey (ed.). Oxford: Blackwell Publishing, 2005, p. 132.

Bibliography

Apollodorus' Library and Hyginus' Fabulae: Two Handbooks of Greek Mythology. R. Scott Smith and Stephen M. Trzaskoma (trans.). Indianapolis: Hackett, 2007.

Apuleius, Lucius. *The Golden Ass*. Sarah Ruden (trans.). New Haven: Yale, 2011.

Cacoyannis, Michael. *Iphigenia*., 1977.

Campbell, Caroline. Lecture on Botticelli's Mars and Venus. National Gallery, 2017. Sandro Botticelli: Venus and Mars in Renaissance Florence. (https://www.youtube.com/watch?v=jNkHq6QXX30.)

Eliot, T. S. 'The Waste Land', in *Modernism: An anthology*. Lawrence Rainey (ed.). Oxford: Blackwell Publishing, 2005, p. 132.

Farrell, Joseph. 'Apuleius and the Classical Canon'. Scholarly Commons, University of Pennsylvania, n.d.

Flaccus, Valerius. *The Argonautica*. J. H. Mozley (ed.) Cambridge: Harvard University Press, 1936.

Hamilton, Edith. *The Roman Way*. New York: W.W. Norton, 2017.

Hejkuk, Julia Dyson. 'Ovid and Religion', *A Companion to Ovid*. Peter E. Knox (ed.). Blackwell Publishing, 2009, pp. 45–58.

Kingsley, Charles. *The Heroes*. Cambridge: Macmillan, 1859.

Marlow, Christopher. *Plays of Christopher Marlowe*. London: Dent, 1909.

Ogden, Daniel. *Perseus*. London: Routledge, 2008.

Ovid, Publius. *The Fasti*. A. J. Boyle and R. D. Woodard (trans.) London: Penguin, 2000.

Ovid, Publius. *The Fasti, Book 3*. James Frazer (trans.). The Theoi Texts Library. (Online: https://www.theoi.com/Text/OvidFasti3.html.)